E-Qual-ity Education

In North Carolina

Among Negroes

By

Hugh Victor Brown

Published 1964

IRVING-SWAIN PRESS, Inc.

303 SOUTH EAST STREET

RALEIGH, NORTH CAROLINA

THE HONORABLE TERRY SANFORD
Governor of North Carolina

"I believe the term, Quality Education, was first used in an address I made to women of the Greensboro area during the first primary in 1960. Of course, our point in talking about Quality Education was that North Carolina needed not only universal education, but needed also the highest quality of education possible."

E-Qual-ity Education In
North Carolina Among Negroes

HUGH VICTOR BROWN

DEDICATION

This work is dedicated to my first wife, Alice Harper Brown, because of her sterling qualities as a teacher of teachers during the resurgence in teacher training under E. C. Brooks, A. T. Allen, and N. C. Newbold and because of the personal inspiration she displayed in my behalf during the early years of my stewardship in education.

Acknowledgement

I am especially grateful to the workers at the State Archives, the State Library, the Richard B. Harrison Library in Raleigh, and the Goldsboro Public Library in Goldsboro for the valuable assistance given me during my researches.

To Mrs. Dorothy W. Hardy, Guidance Counsellor at Dillard High School, for the original reading and correction; N. A. Stitt and Mrs. Thelma Smith, teachers at Dillard High School, who did the typing of the manuscript; Dr. Charles A. Lyons, Executive Secretary of the N. C. Teachers Association and Dr. Lafayette Parker, its current president, who read some of the chapters; and finally to Dr. J. W. Seabrook, President Emeritus of Fayetteville State College, who read every line of the manuscript for final appraisal, I am deeply grateful, I wish also to acknowledge the dedicated men, Superintendents of Goldsboro Schools, under whom I served: O. A. Hamilton, Ray Armstrong (both retired) and N. H. Shope.

My profoundest hope is that the work will find its way into every school and library, as well as into many homes, and will inspire a perpetuation of the history now being made and, more importantly, will seriously challenge youth to burgeon out the best there is in them that they may make the best possible contribution to humanity.

HUGH VICTOR BROWN
Goldsboro, North Carolina
1 9 6 4

Contents

E-Qual-ity Education In North Carolina Among Negroes

CHAPTER I

Pages 17 - 30

Foundation Stones: Administrations of Calvin Wiley, 1866; S. S. Ashley, 1868-71.

CHAPTER II

Pages 31 - 38

Administration of Alexander McIver, 1871-1874.

CHAPTER III

Pages 39 - 48

Administrations: Stephen D. Pool, John Pool, and J. C. Scarborough, 1874-1885.

CHAPTER IV

Pages 49 - 61

Administration of Sidney M. Finger, 1885-1893.

CHAPTER V

Pages 62 - 70

Second Administration of J. C. Scarborough, 1893-1897.

PREFACE

E-QUAL-ITY EDUCATION IN NORTH CAROLINA AMONG
NEGROES

The reason why this book had to be written was perhaps an obsession of the author; of him only, in the light of the psuedonym chosen for the title. The implication is upon the word *equal* and partially upon the word *quality;* two descriptive adjectives one of which has characterized educational progress race-wise in the past — the other which presently is motivating the forces of education in general.

There is no implication of equal education of a prior era — though, as the book will show — tremendous strides have been made in that direction; and as for Quality Education, the implication is plainly one of serious effort to induce its advocates to "Burgeon out the best that lies within" to the end that the utmost needs of humanity may be met.

A previous work, *A History of the Education of Negroes in North Carolina,* was written by this author, that the unique struggle of a people just out of bondage might be preserved for posterity. Some of that history, of course, had been recorded. Much of it, particularly as it concerned the work of education, had been omitted.

The present work, though not a sequel to the former, is an enlargement thereupon and is designed to show in a progressive manner, the gradual strides toward equality in the past and the efforts to attain superior quality of the present among educators and their products. The exploits of our pioneers who blazed the educational trails of Reconstruction as well as those many dedicated souls of the new era must not be lost to coming generations.

We cannot; we would not turn the clock back, but recorded history has been the light by which our feet are guided.

Without the slightest feeling of prejudice, this work is beamed toward progress of the Negro, although that progress cannot be wholly divorced from the activities played by North Carolinians in general. Without the legislative acts of the State and the statesmanship of many consecrated individuals of the dominant race, it would have been impossible to make the progress accorded the Negro.

It is the aim of the author to record the good as well as to recognize the inequities from the time of Superintendent Calvin H. Wiley's administration in 1865-67 to that of our present administration. It is likewise the hope of the author that every citizen, white and Negro, will read and assess the record as it is shown in these pages.

Introduction To

"E-Qual-Ity Education"

With Respect To Negro Education In North Carolina

Equality has ever been the strivings of humanity. Even in Biblical history brothers killed and robbed, as in the case of Cain and Abel, Jacob and Esau — all because of equality. The word is closely akin to freedom and brotherhood. "Liberty, Equality, Fraternity" was the motto of the French Revolution. But, equality is essentially a relative term. Individuals are neither equally tall nor equally heavy; neither equally poor nor equally rich. But by Jefferson's philosophy, "All men are equally endowed by their Creator with life, liberty and the pursuit of happiness"; and so should it be.

Equal education, race-wise, in North Carolina, or anywhere else, has proved a costly venture because it has been accompanied with a separateness which, from the beginning of Negro education, has plagued the consciences of the liberal elements to this day. Costly as it has been for nearly a century, separateness is still essentially the practice, if not the rule of the power structure in the State. Equality, however imperceptible it might seem, is moving definitely in the right direction. Especially is this true with regard to teachers' salaries in public schools which are now equal and in buildings and equipment which are far less unequal than was the case a decade or so ago.

Liberal elements in North Carolina began the long stride toward equality in the first official act, race-wise which was adopted and ratified March 10, 1866, just one year after the close of the Civil War. This act of the Legislature struck out the words "such as were white" from the Code of 1854 which apprenticed destitute white orphans to masters or mistresses who were empowered to teach such destitute orphans to read and write and to learn a trade. The act of 1866 removed the provision," as were white," thus placing the colored apprentice on an equal footing with a white apprentice.[1]

Equality of opportunity in the mid-Twentieth Century has perhaps been more tense than during the late Nineteenth and early Twentieth. It has assumed a recently discovered concept — a situation in which it appears that qualification of accomplishment is the expedient if not the essential "road block" in economic advancement of Negroes. It involves the seriousness of purpose of Negro youth and even of adults in recognizing and preparing for the changes which the present age has adopted.

---

[1]Noble, M. C. S., *History Of Public Schools Of North Carolina*, P. 274.

Prior to the era of automation, more Negroes were employed in the industrial economy of the State and the Nation; especially so in the many trades which, almost unnoticed by Negro educators, gradually gave way to automation for which industrial education, as pursued in Negro institutions, had hardly kept pace. In addition, the expansion of transportatino which had seen Negroes, in nearly every capacity short of conductors and engineers, eliminated as firemen on diesel locomotives, bus operators, air plane pilots; indeed in the operation of most of the heavy construction implements Negroes were suddenly relegated to the "pick and shovel" jobs with correspondingly small pay.

Negro institutions, like Hampton and Tuskegee, which once had supplied the market with expert tradesmen and agriculturists, began de-emphasizing agriculture and trade training in favor of liberal arts and teacher training. Some Negro institutions are pursuing some degree of industrial education in technology and engineering, but the emphasis has hardly approached that of the trade and agricultural theory and practice that attracted so many students to Hampton and Tuskegee prior to World War I.

When the idea of public sponsored industrial education arose for the purpose of training individuals for automation, Negroes suddenly found themselves omitted from industrialization. In his effort to obtain employment in modern industry, he was refused for lack of training. When he applied for the training at industrial centers, he was told that there were no jobs for which he could be trained. It amounted to a vicious circle which liberal leaders, white and Negro, are now trying to circumvent.

Another phase of this concept of inequality is found in the absence of Negroes employed in government positions as clerks or in other appointive roles where lack of qualification is not the real reason. According to the report of the Civil Rights Commission as of July, 1960, in the State Office of the N. C. Employment Security Commission at Raleigh, there were only ten Negro employees as follows: one maid, three elevator operators, five janitors, and two janitor messengers. There were no employees above the rank of janitor messenger, which means no typists, stenographers, clerks, bookkeepers, accountants, or persons in administrative or executive capacity. The commission with a budget (1960) of $5½ million all of which came from the Federal Government, had a total of 945 white and 51 non-white employees throughout the State.[2]

In 1963 James T. Taylor, a Negro retired college professor, was appointed to an executive position with the Employment Security Commission. The Governor of the State, Terry Sanford, has strongly urged fair consideration of qualified Negroes in all phases of employment and has appointed a "Good Neighbor Council" to promote fair employment practices.

---

[2]North Carolina Advisory Commission, *Civil Rights Report*, 1959-62, p. 70.

In many cities in North Carolina and in other states of the South, Negroes are strenuously protesting unequal treatment of their race through non-violent means, "picketting" and "selective buying", all of which are designed to attack the consciences of the ruling majority to the end that the evils of inequality will vanish and all men enjoy the blessings of liberty upon which our nation was founded.

The second phase of the problem which we fear may be neglected in the Negro's zeal to focus attention upon inequalities concerns the Negro's own attitude toward meeting the terms of equality — the other side of the subject of this book: Quality Education. The Negro cannot forever rely wholly or in part upon the "hue and cry of discrimination", however sinister it may be. He cannot rise by "burying his talent in the sand", discrimination, notwithstanding; but must "Burgeon out the best there is in him" for "If a person can write a better story book, make a better horse shoe nail, or build a better mousetrap, even though he live in the midst of the forest, the world will make a beaten path to his door".

Quality Education, in my book, is no new gimmick. It is as old as education itself. It is an old program with a new name and a new emphasis. The history of education in North Carolina is rich with names of dedicated souls who laid an enduring foundation upon which to-day's educators are building. Who can devaluate the teachings of such pioneers as Calvin Wiley, James Y. Joyner, S. G. Atkins, E. E. Smith, P. W. Moore, E. C. Brooks, N. C. Newbold or Annie W. Holland and many others less well known educators of an earlier era?

The author thoroughly subscribes to Governor Sanford's program of "Quality Education" as a positive means to awaken in youth a strong sense of their own responsibilities and possibilities in meeting the needs of the present age and those of the future.

Governor Jonathan Worth had his "New Birth of Education" in 1868; Governor Aycock had his "Universal Education" in 1900; and Governor Sanford "may profit by their example."

What do we understand by "Quality Education"? I asked some of my former associates to write me their views. Together with what Superintendent Charles F. Carroll wrote, here is what they say:

> Quality Education to me means simply making every moment of your school life count in a profitable way — developing good study habits — exploring — evaluating — and accepting the fact that there is so much to learn — and learn it.
>
> Walter A. Foster, Principal
> East End Elementary School
> Goldsboro

> True — Essential — Important. These words to me express the basis for considering the understanding and meaning of quality. When these simple terms are applied to Education, they suggest and strongly urge me to focus my

13

interest and my work on those things which will give the best and strongest support to educational training. Reading, writing, and mathematics still represent the heart of any educational program. A Quality Program should help to insure the highest caliber of work in all areas, but especially in the basic courses and subjects.

John H. Wooten, Sr., Principal
Dillard High School
Goldsboro

An opportunity to learn is the birthright of every American child — a promise that should be fulfilled by our nation's schools, both public and private. The extent to which the school prepares every child passing through its doors for living within the framework of American ideal-ogies, sustained by religious practices, that create moral stamina and democratic beliefs, determine whether or not we can pride ourselves on having "Quality Education."

This term, "quality," as applied to education, simply means helping the child to develop to his fullest potentials; taking the God given talent and multiplying it ten-fold dimensions; teaching him to respect himself and the rights of others, and exploring his talents so that he can utilize them in making wise choices so that he can make a worth-while contribution to our American society.

A. C. Crowder, Principal
Greenleaf School
Goldsboro

The single agent in defining Quality Education is the energetic, versatile, well-tempered teacher, who has built-in educational progressions and is prepared maturally and professionally in many areas of specialty; endowed with various techniques and uses of media in the art of teaching and developing children, which eliminate mediocrity and classroom keeping, and which produce vigorous classroom application known as Quality Education.

Charles I. Bland, Principal
School Street School
Goldsboro

Quality Education, when reduced to the simplest terms is that which accrues from the confrontation of a knowl-edgeable, stimulating, and compassionate teacher and a will-ing and inquisitive pupil using subject matter as a means and not as an end in itself.

Charles F. Carroll, State Superintendent
Department of Public Instruction
Raleigh

Why are we so presently concerned with Quality Education? Is it that through increased emphasis on all phases of education we hope the schools will turn out youngsters who are able to find worthwhile places for themselves in our society?

If this is true, guidance — the process of helping students set reasonable and worthwhile goals for themselves and follow through on these goals — is an integral part of education.

For Quality Education to exist in any school, there must be teachers who are vitally concerned with helping EACH student choose from the educational offerings those experiences which will help HIM develop HIS potential to the maximum. This is guidance — guidance which should demand attention in every school program.

> Dorothy W. Hardy, Guidance Counselor
> Dillard High School
> Goldsboro

With deep appreciation to these fine educators for their clarifying statements on Quality Education, the stage is well set for the developing story of educational progress with respect to Negroes in North Carolina. With no sinister implications, comparisons between the races must be shown. Such will make the story all the more remarkable as progress in comparisons likewise is also shown in Equal as well as in Quality Education.

No two people will describe Quality Education in the same manner; yet all that may be said, no matter in what quality of terms, means simply that Quality Education is the serious business of the parent, the teacher, and the pupil in a profound partnership dedicated to the highest achievement of which each is capable.

Chapter I

Foundation Stores Of Equal And Quality Education

Organized education in North Carolina, as far as Negroes are concerned, had its beginning almost incidentally as thousands of demoralized Negroes followed the conquering armies of the North when the Civil War was drawing to its close. The situation gave rise to the formation of the Freedmen's Bureau, originally called "Bureau of Refugees and Abandoned Lands".

This story has its beginning in the Administration of Calvin H. Wiley, who was State Superintendent of Public Instruction before and during the Civil War which had stripped the schools of most of the male teachers, chief educators of the time; women not having come into the equation of equality, politically nor education-wise. However, the war had forced them to assume teaching duties as well as many other duties which ordinarily belonged to men.

The financial basis for the support of education, The Literary Fund, had amounted to nearly two million dollars, but most of this had been swept away in the wake of the devastating war. Yet during the period, with 65,000 white children in the schools, Wiley with support of the Press insisted that the schools be kept in operation. "The Children of the State must be taught to read, war or no war," said the CHARLOTTE DEMOCRAT.[1]

Wiley was a literary man of one idea, and even in the midst of war, thought only of what had been North Carolina's supreme need — the education of all the people. It was only this single-mindedness of his which saved the schools from utter abandonment.

"As the war went on women gave themselves with all their enthusiasm to the cause of the South, overseeing the (n)egroes at home or doing field work themselves where, as in the majority of cases, there were no (n)egroes, and so kept the system going. It was a frightful responsibility, but they lived up to it splendidly supported by the (n)egroes who, wherever Federal troops did penetrate, displayed a loyalty and devotion which could scarcely be surpassed."

"Unprotected women were safe in their care and the later South owes a debt of gratitude which Reconstruction, even if the (n)egro had been responsible — and he was not — could in no wise cancel."[2]

---

[1] Hamilton, J. G. Roulhack *History of North Carolina*, Vol. III, pp. 347 f.

[2] *Ibid.*, p. 55

One of Wiley's strong hopes of arousing the people's interest and concern for education was publicity — use of open letters in the newspapers and addressed to the Governor of the State, as there were no prior reports made to the people except some annual statement of disbursements of funds and messages of the Governor. Wiley's was the first separate and distinct printed matter giving official information about schools. Almanacs failed to give such information, so Wiley published a school almanac. It said little about the need for teachers, but much about the type of person to be employed. Only teachers should be employed as had morals above reproach and whose lives illustrated the beauties of a heart disciplined to good.

Wiley believed in teachers' associations. A convention was held in Goldsboro as early as 1856 and was attended by many teachers and friends of education. The next year it met in Salisbury. Some of the objectives of the convention were: to disseminate facts and figures about education in the State; to bring together and unite in bonds of professional interest and good feeling of all teachers, college professors, and active friends of education; to increase in those who should attend, their knowledge of North Carolina and her various institutions; to lay the foundation of future meetings of a State Convention; and to be a source of recreation and pleasure for those who were generally confined for the greater portion of the time to the unvarying duties of the school room.

The Educational Association of North Carolina was organized at Salisbury in November 1856. Its official organ was "The N. C. Journal of Education". County and district associations, whose chief objectives were improvement of teachers and diffusion of knowedge, were also organized.[3]

Governor Vance and Education During the War

In his message to the Legislature, November 1862, Governor Vance opposed taking the Literary Fund as "Absolute robbery" of the poor school children. Many teachers were working without pay. At the end of 1864, a salary of $25 was almost nothing — about sixty five cents in gold for a month's service.[4]

From 108,938 children in attendance in 1859, the number had dwindled to 35,495 at the close of the war. Wiley reported that the common schools had lived and discharged their useful mission through the gloom and trials of the conflict; and when the last gun was fired, the doors were still open and numbered their pupils by the thousands.

At the Constitutional Convention called by Governor Holden October 2, 1865, Negro citizens asked for the passage of legislation that would be helpful to them in their new condition of freedom and

---

[3]Noble, *Op. Cit.*, p. 147 f.

[4]*Ibid.*, p. 244.

also for the education of their children so as to make them useful citizens.

A committee appointed to study the problem reported January 22, 1866, declared:

> Persons of color are citizens of the State and they ought to have conferred upon them all the privileges of white persons in conducting their suits and the mode of trial by jury.

The committee discussed much legislation designed to give the freedmen equal rights under the law.[5]

We have already chronicled under the introduction to this story the first legislative educational act (1866, qv.) which placed Negro apprentices on the same footing with white apprentices, thus beginning the long struggle for equality which nearly one hundred years later (1963) had not been fully achieved.

M. C. S. Noble, himself a great author and educator, noted in his *History of Public Schools in North Carolina* in 1930 that Rutherford County in the West and Northampton in the East were among those counties of the State whose records show such cases of binding colored orphans to white masters; and some of those colored apprentices, old men and women of recent years and well remembered by persons to-day (1930) were living witnesses of the good faith of those to whom they had been apprenticed.[6]

Historians, like other authors, are sometimes tempted to evaluate past situations in the light of their own feelings and/or prejudices. For example, Noble states that the education of the Negro would have been solved the "right way" if the people of the South had been permitted to solve it from within, even though slowly, rather than by the clumsy harmful manner by strangers who knew nothing of the proper method of achieving the best permanent results in a southern state.

Armed with the license to indulge in evaluating the situation referred to, it must be said by this author that no one living to-day nor at the time of Noble's statement could say with accuracy how justly the education of the ex-slaves would have been resolved if no outside help had come. The impoverished State could not adequately educate the children of the white race. It is to the undying credit of the Peabody Fund, an outside philanthropic agency, that it came to the aid of both whites and blacks. Added to this agency, were the various missionary societies, outside agencies, let alone that of the Freedmen's Bureau, all of which lifted a great burden from the shoulders of the South. Doubtlessly, errors were made on both sides, as might be the case in any post-war situation.

---

[5] *Ibid.*, p. 272.

[6] *Ibid.*, p. 274.

Worth and Wiley on Education

Jonathan Worth was elected Governor of the State in November 1865 and immediately proclaimed the following:

Our University and the Public Schools, institutions which the Constitution wisely enjoins it on us to sustain, have felt the blighting effects of war. I herewith submit the report of the able and indefatigable Superintendent of Public Schools. He has discussed the subject so fully that I need only commend it to your careful consideration. During the past five years education has been sadly neglected. Whatever may be our pecuniary distresses, our youth must be educated. We must sustain our institutions.

In Wiley's last report he defended the Literary Fund against efforts to use it to pay off the State's debt just as he had defended it against use to carry on the war. He recommended that it be used in continuing schools for the next four years — to be paid to those districts in which schools were being taught. This would give money to districts which wanted a school and stimulate a desire for schools in the hitherto backward localities. He also recommended sale of swamp lands to get revenue for schools.

The Legislature of 1866 not only did not listen to Wiley, but abolished the office of Superintendent of Common Schools and that of the Treasurer of the Literary Fund. It made taxation discretionary and left in permissive with the counties to operate schools if they could and desired to do so.[7] One might imagine what schooling Negroes could receive under such conditions if help had not come from unexpected sources.

Thus, by Legislative action, Calvin Wiley, the long time successful and hard working head of the common school system, was handed his "honorable discharge".[8]

The Legislature of 1866-67 authorized towns and cities to establish public school systems to be supported by taxes collected or authorized to be collected for corporate purposes. Provision was made for local trustees and local Boards of Education who could levy and collect a poll tax on every white male over 21 of not over $2 for use of public schools.[9]

S. S. Ashley and Reconstruction

An oddity in early public school administration was that many leading officials were preachers. Wiley had been listed as Reverend C. H. Wiley. The Reverend S. S. Ashley, a native of Massachusetts,

---

[7]Knight, Edgar, *Public Education In North Carolina*, p. 222.

[8]Noble, *Op. Cit.*, p. 274.

[9]Knight, *Op. Cit.*, p. 222.

became the first superintendent of the Reconstruction era and his assistant was the Reverend J. W. Hood, a Negro clergyman who moved to North Carolina from Pennsylvania.

Ashley was elected under a situation which might have been termed explosive; that is, it was during a time of "stress and strain," mingled with politics, selfish interests, ignorance, prejudice, and poverty, in which condition, right and reason might easily be overcome by emotions. So-called "carpet-baggers" had come into the State and, with the aid of ill-advised freedmen, assumed control of the State government. When the Committee on Education of the Constitutional Convention in 1868 adopted amendments providing for the separation of the races in the University and public schools, the radical elements defeated them. Ashley, though not lacking in ability, but full of prejudices which made him narrow, favored mixed schools.

There were several Negroes of ability who were members of the Convention of 1869. Included were Robert Harris, J. W. Hood, both of whom we shall hear more, and A. H. Galloway. The Convention Committee on Education contains no provision for separate schools, but an amendment was offered by Plato Durham, a conservative member of the convention, the following to wit:

> The General Assembly shall provide separate and distinct schools for the black children of the State from those provided for white children.

Another amendment would provide:

> That in all cases where district schools shall be established there shall be ample, sufficient, and complete facilities afforded for the one class as for others and entirely adequate for all; and in all districts where schools are divided the apportionment to each shall be equal.

Both of these amendments were defeated.

The Constitution, adopted out of the Convention of 1867, had been silent on the subject of mixed schools, but the first law passed under it provided for separate schools of 4 months term. The Public School Law of 1869 provided for a State Board of Education and the residue of the Literary Fund was distributed among the counties according to the scholastic population.[10] [11]

Appointment of J. W. Hood, Assistant State Superintendent

The minutes of the State Board on September 23, 1868 stated the following:

---

[10]*Ibid.*, p. 229.

[11]Hamilton, *Op. Cit.*, p. 611 f.

BISHOP JAMES W. HOOD

Assistant Superintendent of Public Instruction in 1869

The interest of Public Common School education requires appointment of an agent who shall act in the capacity of Assistant Superintendent of Public Instruction. Therefore it is ordered that the Reverend J. W. Hood, of Cumberland, be and hereby is appointed said Assistant Superintendent of Public Instruction at an annual salary of $1,250.[12]

The Legislature of 1869 authorized the State Superintendent and Board to organize a system of schools with an appropriation of $100,000 and ordered a census taken.

In appointing J. W. Hood, the only Negro who has ever held the position of Assistant State Superintendent of Public Instruction, Ashley wrote the following:

Deeming it of great importance that the school interests of the colored population of the State be thoroughly investigated, that the numerous and widely scattered schools existing among them should be inspected and such instruction given the people as was needed to prepare them for the introduction of the Public School system, and it was evident that this work could not be accomplished by the Superintendent of Public Instruction without assistance, the Board has secured the services of J. W. Hood to act as agent of the Board and Assistant Superintendent of Public Instruction.

With great skill, fidelity, and industry, Mr. Hood has pursued the work of exploration and investigation. His report is embodied in the report of the Superintendent of Public Instruction. Special attention is asked for it as it presents a more intelligent and complete view of the work of education among the colored population of this State than has yet been given.

—S. S. Ashley[13]

The report of the Reverend J. W. Hood is an interesting and valuable document as it afforded a more satisfactory view of educational work among the colored population.

Schools established under his supervision were sponsored by the American Missionary Association — best known for many decades as the A. M. A. — and the American Union Freedmen's Commission. These organizations not only supplied teachers, but erected buildings and spent $2 to the freedmen's $1 to encourage building.

The citation of this report of Hood is written just as Hood gave it; much written in the present tense and in the style with which Hood wrote. It is placed here because of the importance of the document.

---

[12]Noble, *Op. Cit.*, p. 319.

[13]*North Carolina School Report of* 1869, p. 34.

The early schools reported by Hood are as follows:

1. The Johnson School at Raleigh erected on the A. M. E. lot by the Freedmen's Bureau accommodated 300 pupils.

2. The Washington School in Raleigh entirely under the A. M. A.

3. The Smithfield School, running days and nights, with an enrollment of 125.

4. The Howard School at Fayetteville — "Best in the State"; according to Inspector General Avery.[14] The Bureau had erected a building costing $3,800 on a site costing $140 and furnished at a cost of $400. Enrollment was 300 pupils.

5. Whiteville, a school with 45 pupils.

6. Schools in Wilmington established by the A. M. A. with a total of 750 pupils. The largest of these was the Williston, having over 450 pupils with five departments: primary, intermediate, advanced, normal, and industrial.

7. Colored Elementary Institute, of Wilmington, erected on a site given by the City with a building furnished by the Bureau and accommodating 200 pupils.

8. The Orphans Asylum, situated on Middle Sound with 27 inmates; S. H. Beal, Superintendent.

9. Carteret — All schools under the A. M. A.; the most important being at Beaufort with 425 pupils, 5 teachers, a superintendent and a matron. Each teacher has adult night classes in addition to day duties. The school is well graded and classed. Site owned by colored and building erected by them with assistance from the A. M. A.; property held by a colored Board of Trustees.

I consider Beaufort one of our most highly favored towns — having a permanent school building not controlled by any particular denomination.[15]

10. Morehead City — School tolerably good; also Hall Swamp. Teachers are earnest good men, but have not had that training necessary to fully qualify to teach.

11. A good house at North River and also one at Clumsfoot Creek, but no school due to want of a teacher.

12. Three schools at New River; one at Trent Settlement.

13. New Bern — There are 300 pupils and 3 teachers; school is graded. The Metcalf School is primary with 102 pupils. The intermediate occupies a building erected by the Bureau on a Methodist lot — a very good building, but having been erected for a Church, children have to recite in an undertone. The advanced department occupies the Congregational Church rented by the Bureau. Miss Chloe Merrick is the preceptress. She informs me that she never had to use the rod in her school. If punishment is needed she sends to the parents and will not take them back until the parents correct them,

---

[14]*Ibid.*, p. 18.

[15]*Ibid.*, p. 20.

bring them back to school and she is assured that they will obey. The school has the largest number of advanced pupils in the State.

14. Elizabeth City —The school is supplied by the Union Commission.

Nearly all schools have established temperance societies. Many of the teachers are graduates of northern institutions — men and women who are willing to make any sacrifice for the purpose of elevating a long oppressed and degraded people. The members pledge themselves to abstain from intoxicants, tobacco in every form, and vulgar or profane language.

Schools Established By the Friends Society

These are doing a great work without expectation of reward. The Bible is read without comment, particularly respecting moral character. The Friends have established 37 schools with a pupil enrollment of 2,475.

1. Goldsboro — 280 pupils; Miss Blanche Harris, the preceptress is a graduate of Oberlin College in Ohio. She had been teaching in the South for five or six years and is considered one of our best teachers. The school is graded: primary, intermediate, and advanced. There are three buildings owned by the Friends Society.

2. Mebanesville — a Presbyterian School.

3. Hillsboro — Poorly managed. Hoped a recent change in teacher would improve conditions.

4. Greensboro — a good school.

5. Salisbury — one of the best.

6. Charlotte — one of the largest.

7. Lincolnton — also a large school; 13 in Rowan.

8. Davie and Iredell — there are three schools in Davidson and three in Guilford.

Episcopalian Schools

There are seven of these besides the high school in Raleigh; two in New Bern, one in Raleigh, one in Wilmington, and one in Fayetteville. The discipline in these schools is commendable. The Mission school in Fayetteville is an exception. Order is not one of the ingredients of which this school is composed. The teachers are generally most excellent ladies whose hearts are evidently in the work.

The Bureau has appropriated $5,000 for the erection of a building at Raleigh for a normal school.

Presbyterian Schools

These are making a great effort to establish a system of Parochial schools. They have already established a college at Charlotte with a normal department and are sending out preachers and school teachers for schools of higher grade. Through the Bureau, the Government has appropriated $10,000. The denomination has some very good schools. The largest is at Charlotte. There are five others in Mecklenburg County; three in Cabarrus; three in Rowan; one in Iredell; one in Davie; one in Davidson; one in Guilford; and one in Wilmington.

Private Schools

These are scattered all over the State except beyond the Blue Ridge, where not a single school has been found. There were Sabbath schools at several points and anxiety existed for day schools, but the lack of books and teachers was cause for much complaint.

Some of these are good and some are bad.

Mr. Tupper's school is one of the largest and best in this class and has enrolled 250 pupils; hopes to establish a college. (Beginnings of Shaw University)

The Miles school in Raleigh, held in a Reverend Mr. Warwick's church, later came under the Union Commission which also sponsored the Clinton School at Concord, a school at Oxford, one at Bethel Hill, and one at Louisburg. Edenton supported two good private schools, Hertford one, Washington one, Tarboro one, and Kinston one. There were only a few counties east of the Blue Ridge with no school at all.

A very large number of these schools were held in buildings which were but a small improvement on being out of doors. To name the places where freedmen have put up these rude shanties would be to speak of the largest portion of these private schools. So anxious were they to have schools that, where they could do no better, they would pile up rough logs and cover them with rived boards. The contentment of the children was astonishing in these uncomfortable houses and, poor as they were, these buildings were often subjected to the enmity of the whites and burned down.

Hood's summary, submitted to Superintendent Ashley April 22, 1869, just four years following the close of the war, is a great tribute to the ambitions of the ex-slaves and of the activities of the various societies to establish schools for the colored children.

Summary

	No. of Schools	Teachers	Pupils
A. M. A. and Freedmen's Union	19	68	2,840
The Friends Society	29	40	2,425
Episcopalian Commission	6	11	600
Presbyterian	16	21	1,100
Private	82	84	4,861
Total	152	224	11,826

A note added to Hood's summary stated that since April 1869, the number of schools had reached 257 and pupils 15,647. This was due to normal classes generally established in the larger towns during the previous winter. These so-called normal classes supplied the best teachers.

If sufficient encouragement can be given to normal classes, there will be a much larger increase of this class of teachers.

Hood urged that the proposed "Colored Department" at the University be opened as a normal school, but, in his words:

As there appears to be an objection amounting to a prohibition of the use of the unoccupied buildings at Chapel Hill by colored pupils, perhaps the best that can be done for the present is to establish normal schools at several different places in the State, selecting those places that have the largest number of good material.

The Freedmen's Bureau, according to the Hood report, was spending $1,700 monthly for the support of colored schools aside from large amounts for buildings and repairs.

From all reports Hood seemed to be a real professional who recognized the importance of teachers' meetings as a means to motivate improvement. His first educational meeting held during the summer of 1869 was well attended.[16]

Concerning Hood's observation relative to the "Colored Department" at the University, Noble records that at the reopening of the University in 1868, Chief Justice Richmond M. Pearson had offered a resolution that would provide for the education of colored students at some place other than at Chapel Hill, seat of the University or its vicinity. His resolution would provide a Department of the University and upon the plan set out in the donation of the land scrip by Act of Congress and "exclusively for the use of pupils of color." This resolution was adopted November 20, 1868. At the meeting of the University trustees in January, 1869 an elaborate plan was adopted for a department of colored students. This would include such instruction as was regarded necessary to train intelligent agriculturists and mechanics; and offered such classical studies as may be suited to fit pupils for the University.[17]

This appears to have been a most liberal proposal which might have been a solid foundation for equal educational opportunity of that era and for quality education of the present era (the 1960's), but the fearful Legislature failed to provide the department of colored students.

A new plan was proposed in 1869 to set up a colored department which should have a principal and as many assistants as might

---

[16]*Ibid.*, pp. 25, 26.

[17]Noble, *Op. Cit.*, p. 340 f.

be necessary — a model farm, work shops, etc. for the education of colored pupils. Approval of this plan was included in the message of Governor Holden to the Legislature:

> The Trustees will organize the Colored Department as rapidly as their means will permit. This department is not only a matter of justice, but of necessity.[18]

Like the previous body, the Legislature of 1869 paid no heed to the Governor's request and left the matter of Negro education to later administrations, thus losing valuable time in the State's recognition and acceptance of the responsibility toward equal education for all its citizens.

It is difficult to evaluate a situation with unprejudiced minds, not having lived in it; or to assess the blame for inaction without danger of injustice. But with a State caught within cross currents of political manueverings and fraught with fear of its own acts, there is small wonder that it made any progress at all.

However, serious efforts to move ahead into a real school system were centered around certain objectives which we shall endeavor to explain.

County Examiners

The forerunner of our present system of county school administration was the County Examiner. The Public School Law of 1869 provided that a county examiner be appointed — a man of good moral character and of suitable attainments to examine applicants to teach and to report annually to the State Superintendent of Public Instruction.[19]

School Census

The first school census in which colored children were included was taken in 1869. It showed a total of 223,815 white and 106,766 colored children between the ages of six and tweny-one. The leading counties, as far as colored children were concerned, were Wake with 4,094; New Hanover with 4,020; and Craven with 3,237. Wayne Couny reported 2,159 colored children. The low report showed: Clay County with 60 (no schools for either race); Jackson 90; Madison 89; Mitchell 74; and Watauga 65. Onslow and Edgecombe counties failed to report.

General Sentiment

The status of the times, though critical, demanded some sort of a system of schools that would include the education of colored child-

---

[18] *Ibid.*, p. 340 f.

[19] *Report State Superintendent* 1869, p. 22.

ren. One of the most serious hindrances was the lack of funds to operate schools and another was the sentiment of a great number of people. Aside from the residue of the Literary Fund, the net proceeds accruing to the State from fines, penalties and forfeitures became a part of the State Public School Fund. In addition to these funds three-fourths of a poll tax became a part of the school funds.

From Ashley's report to Governor Holden in 1869 is the following important statement:

> The establishment of an efficient Public School System is demanded by the people — a necessity — not only the public voice, but the public good requires it. Without such a system, immigrants will shun the State and its valuable, intelligent, enterprising will flee its borders. Establishment of a respectable system demands a larger appropriation . . . 350,000 children to be instructed. Surely the State can afford $2 per head! The State may be poor, but a poor State can, least of all, afford to be ignorant. Poverty without intelligence becomes degradation, misery, crime; no State can afford such results.[20]

In the fall of 1870, seventy county examiners reported to Ashley on conditions as, "Obstacles in the Way": lack of money to build and repair; stubborn opposition to tax, especially from the farmers record of low prices; lack of competent teachers, especially, colored; much native prejudice against colored education; (n)egro committeemen, etc. One examiner reported that there were so few colored children in a certain western county that to provide for them in a separate school was almost as difficult as providing for the great number in eastern counties. From Columbia Township in Transylvania County came a report: "No school had been established for colored children because we could not procure teachers, but hope that the school would be in successful operation next year". Alaska Township in Macon County gave this report: "There is one female colored child in this township. We will make arrangements for the instruction privately."

In many western counties no colored children of school age were reported. This was also true in some near eastern counties. For instance, in Waccamaw Township of Brunswick County which had a large colored population, the report showed only nine colored children and stated that it was impracticable to provide a school for them.

Ashley wrote the Attorney-General on February 5, 1870 asking if such children could be excluded from attending any free school where no provision for their instruction was made. No reply came from the Attorney-General to his question.[21]

---

[20]*Ibid.*, p. 53.

[21]Noble, *Op. Cit.*, p. 321.

Aside from the outside help of the Peabody Fund,[22] other sources are credited with aiding both white and colored schools. In 1867 the Soldiers Memorial Society of Boston and the American Unitarian Association sent a Miss Amy M. Bradley to Wilmington. She was a woman of far more than ordinary gifts, possessed of unbounded faith and energy and the priceless gift of tact.

Realizing that more good could be accomplished by the training of white teachers, she established two grammar schools and later, through the generosity of a Mrs. Hemenway of Boston, a normal school was built which became the city's high school out of which grew the city's school system.

Many of Miss Bradley's pupils became enthusiastic teachers and her influence still lives. (1914). Although Hamilton did not specify what aid Miss Bradley gave to establishing colored schools, he does mention the enlightening report of J. W. Hood (qv.) and states that by far the best work among colored people was done by schools conducted under the various associations.[23]

The Legislature of 1870, like the several previous ones, hardly seemed to appreciate efforts of the Superintendent of Public Instruction, for it reduced Ashley's salary and in 1871 chagrined at the loss of prestige, he resigned to accept a position at Straight University, a Negro institution in New Orleans.

Summary of the Chapter

The acts of three men, Wiley, Ashley, and Hood more than those of any other, best epitomize the substance of this chapter. Calvin Wiley's dedication to the schools kept them alive despite the ravages of the Civil War. S. S. Ashley, upon the ruins of the Literary Fund and the apathy of the people, rebuilt a system of public schools. J. W. Hood, with tireless energy, great ability, and indefatigable courage motivated the establishing of many schools for colored children. These men stand out prominently in this epic establishing the foundation upon which equal opportunity and quality performance were to be erected in the education of Negroes in North Carolina.

---

[22]Brown, H. V., *A History Of The Education Of Negroes In North Carolina*, p. 29.

[23]Hamilton, *Op. Cit.*, p. 613.

Chapter II

The Administration Of Alexander McIver
1871-74

Upon the resignation of S. S. Ashley in 1871, Governor Caldwell appointed Alexander McIver State Superintendent of Public Instruction. McIver, a Republican in politics, was not the dynamic type for the critical times according to Historian Noble.

A leader of strategic ability and an advocate of persuasive powers as a public speaker was needed to lead men out of the bad humor they were in and unite them in an enthusiastic support of the public schools.

Yet his reports to the Governor display an enormous amount of knowledge and wisdom which, had it been accepted by the dubious legislatures, might have forged the State ahead in the progress of education. School houses and school teachers, he said, should be the best in the State. Teachers' certificates should be made to indicate with certainty that the holder is of good moral character, that he is familiar with all branches required to be taught, and that he has been trained to teach and is in all respects fitted for the profession.

The system should be practical, providing for agricultural and industrial pursuits — a system of public instruction which is to permeate all classes and conditions of society; which is to influence the manners, the habits, the thoughts, and opinions of the young, the middle-aged, and the old; and to reach every man, woman, and child.

Questioned as to how the low status of the State's debt would fit into the scheme of education, he responded: "Educate the people and they will pay the State debt".

Unlike Ashley, McIver was no advocate of "mixed schools". His report does not indicate anything of the role of J. W. Hood, who had been Ashley's assistant superintendent, but it must be assumed that Hood's tenure ended with that of Ashley's. A letter from an unknown, quoted below, indicates that the question of Negro education was presented to McIver.

As to the African race, the results of education is doubtful; but in this age of the world, the experiment must be tried in good faith. While I think no system of instruction will ever lift the African to the high spheres of educated mind, yet LET THE ROLE BE PLAYED FAIRLY;

and if the results should not be commensurate with the demands of Christian civilization, the error will not be ours.[1]

In his efforts to make some progress in public school education, McIver was not only frustrated by legislative acts, but by court decisions. The Supreme Court in January 1871 declared that schools were not a "necessary expense" of county government which decision had the effect of nullifying the school system of 1868-69. The fact was brought out that although there was a clause in the Constitution requiring the county commissioners, under penalty, to maintain public schools for four months every year, there was also a clause which made it impossible for a county to do so; viz.,

> No county, city, or town shall levy any tax, except for the necessary expenses thereof, unless by a majority vote of the people.

In the eyes of the Supreme Court, the school tax was not a "necessary expense" within the meaning of the Constitution and could be levied and collected only by a vote of the people. However, the Legislature could levy a tax and the Constitution makes it the duty of the Legislature to do so.

The General Assembly of 1871 could either levy a tax upon the property of the State to support and carry on a system as it was or modify it and make it conform to the wishes and will of the people. Such an amendment to levy a tax upon the property of the State to support the school system as existed was voted down by a large majority.

A new proposal made by McIver was finally adopted in February 1872. His proposal was framed upon the idea that education was not a charity for the poor, but a debt the State owed to the young; that all children of the State had an equal right to the privileges of an education and that it was the duty of the State to maintain that right.

McIver's idea was that the public schools should take the place of the private schools and that all primary and grammar schools in the State should become the public schools. The idea that free schools were intended only for the poor was a misconception of the design of public instruction. "The poor indeed", he said, "should be admitted to the public schools, free of charge, but the system should embrace all upon equal terms."

The new law provided and encouraged organizations of teachers' associations and institutes for the improvement of instruction. The Peabody Fund afforded $50 to assist in each teachers' institute.

McIver was also an advocate of compulsory attendance — (the term then used was compulsory education). Quoting from a Dr. Palmer, McIver wrote:

> Compulsory Education is a public benefit — a protection of children against the ignorance and selfishness of parents.

---

[1]Noble, *Op. Cit.*, p. 354.

He had garnered information from countries in Europe to show the favorable effects of compulsory education in European countries. From Baden, Germany:

> In 1854 there were 1426 prisoners; in 1871, there were only 691. Marriage augmented, illegitimate births diminished, and thefts decreased from 1,009 to 400. The number of indigents declined one-fourth.

Similar results he said had been noted in Switzerland. Compulsory education is ancient and noble in origin. It dates back to the time of Solon and is incorporated in the legislation of the most enlightened nations of Europe. By the laws of Solon, "Every man should have his son instructed in music and gymnastics. By the laws of Lycurgus of Sparta, the State took the education of the children of his courtiers to attend them." In 1554 Martin Luther said: "If a state in time of war can compel its citizens to take up the sword, has it not still more power and is it not its duty to compel them to instruct their children since we are all engaged in a most serious war, waged with the spirit of evil which rages in our midst seeking to depopulate the State of its virtuous men?"

McIver surveyed the status of compulsory education in the United States which showed progressive steps in other states which convinced him of the necessity of adopting compulsory education in North Carolina.

The census of 1870 showed 38,647 whites and 40,955 colored (10 to 15 years of age) unable to read and write; and over 10 years of age, 191,961 white and 205,032 colored, plus 679 Indians or a total of 397,690 illiterates in the State.[2]

The above figures on illiteracy and the following on enrollment must have plagued the very soul of the State Superintendent. At the close of his first biennium, the census of school children showed 234,846 white children of which only 119,083 were enrolled and 123,088 colored of which only 55,000 were enrolled. It is readily seen that not half the children of school age were enrolled in school. The average length of the term was 10 weeks and the proportion of persons (6 to 21) not in school was so large that the case of public education seemed almost hopeless. Some measure of financial relief came from the Peabody Fund which in the period from 1863 to 1876 made grants of from $2,700 to $8,050.

McIver was defeated for reelection in 1872 by James Reid who died before assuming the office. Kemp Battle was appointed to the superintendency, but McIver refused to relinquish the position on the grounds that no successor had qualified for the position and he was sustained by the Supreme Court. He served until the end of the biennium.[3]

---

[2] *Biennial Report* 1870-71, p. 3 f.

[3] Hamilton, *Op. Cit.*, p. 616.

33

McIver's report for the biennium ending in 1872 showed a total of $155,393.96 expended for public schools, but that reports from the counties were so incomplete that it was difficult to get an accurate statement of educational conditions. It appeared that the sum of $71,861.35 was paid for the education of the whites in 46 counties and the sum of $27,256.16 for Negroes in the same counties. A law of 1872 provided the sum of $50 to each institute for the improvement of teachers. A like amount was appropriated by the Peabody Fund.

According to Historian Knight, nothing in educational circles was more confusing and alarming than the fear of mixed schools despite the fact that the School Law provided for separation of the races in the public schools. At the height of the Civil Rights agitation in Congress in 1874, McIver wrote:

> No legislation in favor of mixed schools has ever been attempted in this state. Public sentiment on this subject is all one way. Opposition to mixed schools is so strong that if the people are free to choose between mixed schools and no schools, they will prefer the latter.

With educational interest already at a very low ebb, the Civil Rights agitation did not serve to improve it, but the Educational Convention of 1873 had served to bolster the sagging sentiment. The Lexington Normal School of the Davidson County Board of Education, under a special act of the Legislature had annual sessions of 25 days instruction to teachers of both races. In 1874 the enrollment was 36 white and 35 colored teachers instructed separately.

The year ending 1874 showed the Educational Fund amounting to $496,405.23; paid for white education, $182,646 and $77,615.25 paid for Negro education. The school population (the census) at the end of McIver's tenure was 242,768 white and 127,192 colored children, with corresponding enrollments of 119,083 and 55,000.

One of the most progressive recommendations made by McIver before leaving office was that of appointing experienced teachers to be county superintendents in every county.[4] As pointed out before, many of the heads of educational administration had been preachers. Aside from this fact, the county examiner might be a lawyer, a business man, or any politican who needed a job. McIver earnestly thought that the schools should be headed by professionals. Said he:

> If an edifice is to be erected, we put an architect in charge. His superior skill is seen in every part of the building. So a skillful, experienced teacher at the head of the school system in a county, would very soon impress evidences   and leave marks of his knowledge and experience in every school house and district in the county. No one should be eligible for this office except a practical teacher of high standing in his profession. It is due to the teachers that

---

[4]Knight, *Op. Cit.*, p. 251.

the office of county superintendent be confined to them. They are the only class that are qualified for the work and the very fact of confining the office to them would elevate the profession of teaching.[5]

From this philosophy on professional administration of the schools, it appears that McIver was ahead of his time for as late as the 1920's, some of the counties still had ministers to head the schools as superintendent. Yet it must be said that many of the early educators, who were also ministers, exerted a wholesome influence upon character building among students.

McIver was also a great advocate of grade schools which had been authorized for every city or town of more than 2,000 inhabitants, if approved by vote of the people. This would provide a school term in such cities or towns for 10 months. Obstacles in the way of the bill to establish graded schools stemmed largely from the unwillingness of some citizens to have their children come in contact with children whose moral training had been neglected. McIver argued that instead of weakening, the graded school would strengthen the moral character of every child. It would annihilate caste and aristocracy among children.

> The rich and the poor sit side by side in the same class under the same instruction and amenable to the same discipline. Intelligence, honesty, and integrity are the tools by which all are tried and by which every one must stand or fall.

The first graded school was established at Greensboro in 1870, followed by Charlotte in 1873, and several other cities after McIver's administration.[6]

The Legislature of 1873 authorized the appointment of three county examiners in place of one as provided by the Law of 1869. But the lack of power in the county examiners to do anything by way of leadership was a great draw back to the schools.[7]

Outside Aid: Peabody Fund, Friends Association

A partial report of Dr. Barnas Sears, Agent of the Peabody Fund in 1871-72 showed liberal funds used to aid schools in Wilmington, New Bern, Washington, Durham Creek, Beaufort, Smithfield, Kenansville, Hillsboro, Carthage, Kinston, Plymouth, Charlotte, and others. The Baltimore Friends Association aided in setting up a large number of schools and held institutes for teacher improvement. A model farm near High Point had been established by this association.

---

[5]*Biennial Report* 1873-74, Doc. 5, p. 58.

[6]*Biennial Report* 1872-73, Doc. 5, p. 23.

[7]Noble, *Op. Cit.*, p. 372.

Their superintendent was a Mr. Allen Jay. Of the establishment of these schools, McIver wrote:

> While these benefactors recognize the value of education, they also indicate the good will of these authors. They are but so many olive branches held out to the people to unite in building up a prosperity of a common country upon the only basis which it can be done, the education of the people.[8]

While much of the State Superintendent's reports are incomplete, due to the failure of county and other school officials to submit accurate and timely information to the department, McIver reported that public sentiment in favor of education was increasing. Educational associations were being organized in many counties and more people were taking an interest in public schools than formerly. Strict supervision, a better scheme of education, and the employment of a better class of teachers, fewer schools, and better schools all combined were causing obstacles to disappear.

Funds at the end of the biennium, June 30, 1874 were $496,405.23 of which $297,594.85 was expended. The number of white children on the school census was 242,765; colored, 127,192.[9]

One of the most progressive acts of the McIver Administration was the formation of the State Educational Association. Early in 1873, the State Board of Education adopted a resolution calling for a meeting of friends of education. They convened at Raleigh on July 9, 1873 for the purpose of considering and recommending such measures as they deemed advisable for the promotion of education in the State. Teachers and others were invited and the Convention's first act was the organization of the State Educational Association. Resolutions requesting public speakers and the Press to use their influence in behalf of education were adopted. The public was urged to favor the establishment of a four-months school in every district of the State in which should be taught reading, writing, and elementary rules of arithmetic — text books to be furnished by the State Superintendent. (This evidently meant text books selected by the State Superintendent.)[10]

Among the delegates to the Convention mentioned by McIver as being present were Robert Harris and Osborne Hunter, both Negroes. Hunter was listed on the printed program of the Second Annual Convention in 1874 and made a memorable speech which was highly praised by some of the most prominent white delegates.[11]

---

[8]*Biennial Report* 1872-73, Doc. 5, p. 59.

[9]Noble, *Op. Cit.*, p. 368.

[10]*Ibid.*, p. 373 f.

[11]Brown, H. V., *Op. Cit.*, p. 113.

Another act of the first convention was a resolution endorsing "National Aid" to Education — then being discussed in Congress. These discussions and resolutions were helpful to legislators as well as to the public as they strengthened the cause of popular education by giving to the people the names of those citizens who were coming to the front in advocacy of a public educational system convenient to reach every child in the State.[12]

Summary

In McIver's final report, only 73 counties are included, the others neglecting to send in reports. However, the report shows 2,350 public school houses for white and 999 for colored children. Estimating the total from prior reports from the missing counties, McIver placed the number of schools at 2,820 for white and 1200 for colored children; the number of children at 119,083 white and 55,000 colored.

> The State must take charge of these children and place them in schools where their minds can be enlightened and their hearts trained to virtue.[13]

Excerpts from reports coming from some of the counties are interesting as they depict the seriousiness of the times. Robeson County reported that the schools for colored children were generally without teachers and a few white teachers were teaching colored children. There were a few colored teachers who had certificates and were teaching. Stokes County had no colored school for the lack of teachers and children were so scattered that a school could not be made up for them.

Wilson County reported three private institutions: all white. Wilson Collegiate Institute, Wilson Collegiate Seminary, and Staunton (sic) High School. J. W. Farmer, County Treasurer wrote:

> The people of this county have not heretofore taken much interest in public schools, but I think they will have more schools this fall and winter. I believe the people are beginning to take an interest in free public schools.

Mecklenburg County reported a military institute and a female institute.

> The city school was organized a year ago, Reverend J. B. Boone, Superintendent; S. E. Belk, County Treasurer. In the Treasurer's report, July 1, 1874, he has charged himself with $600.00 interest which he received on deposit of school money in the bank. He has heretofore accounted for interest received on deposit of school money, and is the only treasurer in the State who has done so.

---

[12]Noble, *Op. Cit.*, p. 373.

[13]*Biennial Report* 1874, Doc. 5, p. 15.

Forsythe County reported the celebrated "Salem Female Academy," one of the oldest in the State and had over 300 pupils. There were three other flourishing academics in the county with 40 scholars each. M. H. Linville, Chairman of the Board of Examiners wrote:

I am inclined to think the present law would work well if parents and other citizens would do their duty to free schools. As the Constitution declares a 4-months school in every district, our law makers ought to levy a tax on the people of the State sufficient to guarantee the 4-months school. If left to the people to vote, they will vote it down as they have done.

Craven County, The Reverend L. C. Vass, Chairman of the Examiners reported several private schools in New Bern and perhaps others in the County. New Bern Academy was supported by an endowment fund, aid in part by the public school, and by The Peabody Fund. J. C. Harrison, County Register, reported that a lack of good competent school committeemen in some townships has caused schools to be neglected.[14]

Final figures reported by McIver in his last biennial reports are as follows:[15]

Number of white males (6 to 21)	120,484; females	114,362
Number of colored males (6 to 21)	63,148; females	59,940
Enrolled white males	54,033; females	45,220
Enrolled colored males	23,064; females	23,603
Number white male teachers	1,206; females	495
Number colored male teachers	416; females	204

Neither figures for average daily attendance nor percentages were given, but a glance at the comparison between the number of children listed and the number enrolled shows that less than half of the number of children available were enrolled in either white or colored schools.

The next chapter will record the rather tarnised administrations of S. D. Pool and John Pool and the more salient administration of John C. Scarborough.

---

[14] *Ibid.*, p. 81.

[15] *Ibid.*, p. 97.

Chapter III

Administrations Of Stephen D. Pool, John Pool And J. C. Scarborough

Stephen D. Pool assumed the office of State Superintendent of Public Instruction November 19, 1874, succeeding Alexander McIver, who was defeated for reelection. Pool had been the agent for the State Education Association and, upon assuming the office of State Superintendent, began a state-wide canvass in behalf of education. At the same time, under the auspices of the Peabody Fund, he began an examination of those schools which were receiving aid from that fund. He declared people apathetic and public education languishing everywhere — the cause, he said, being sentiment against, hard times, and criticism of his predecessor, Alexander McIver.

By March 17, 1876, Pool renounced any ambition to continue in office and soon thereafter was charged with defaulting Peabody funds. He subsequently resigned the office and promised to rectify his mistake.[1]

On the matter of the irregularities involving the Peabody Fund, Dr. Barnas Sears, its agent, writing from his office in Staunton, Virginia, had this to say:

> The State Superintendent who was chargeable with irregularities — I do not say intentional fraud — in handling of funds, has resigned and no successor has yet been appointed. . . . He spent four months in our service as travelling agent at the recommendation of Governor Graham. His opinion was that we should be MORE rather than LESS rigid in the selection of schools to be aided even those which outwardly conform to our requirements. A school may be unsuccessful either from bad management or from the appointment of incompetent teachers. Whenever this happens, as it sometimes does with schools patronized by us, it tends to impair confidence in the wisdom of our measures . . . .
> We should not relax our requirements, but rather insist more stringently on conformity to the spirit and to the letter of our requirements.

Dr. Sears was profoundly in agreement with the proposal to establish normal schools. Said he:

> Thus far we have felt the want of a good system in North Carolina. I think the other southern states have a better

---

[1]Noble, *Op. Cit.*, p. 375.

school law. If the State will establish one or more normal schools we will cooperate.[2]

John Pool, a cousin of Stephen Pool, was appointed to the Superintendency in July of 1876. His record is based largely upon the statistics gathered by Stephen Pool and upon the recommendation made by McIver relative to the appointment of county superintendents. He served until 1877. No constructive work for education was accomplished under either Stephen Pool or John Pool.

John C. Scarborough

John C. Scarborough was elected State Superintendent in 1877. The Public School Law of 1877 directed a tax of 8⅓c on property and 25c on polls in addition to the state capitation tax for schools, the tax on liquors, fines, forfeitures and penalities which would constitute the total funds for education. It also directed that if funds were not sufficient for a four-months school term in any county, the county commissioners could levy annually a special tax to insure a four-months school, provided it was submitted to the vote of the qualified voters of the county. The law did not make it mandatory, but left it at the discretion of the county commissioners.

School Law of 1877

Perhaps the most important legislative act of Scarborough's administration was that of the establishment of the "Colored Normal School" at Fayetteville on February 20, 1877. In addition, the School Law of 1877 provided for the establishment of a summer normal school at the University and permitted the levying of a special tax by race for the benefit of the schools of either race.

Although Historian Noble called this item of the School Law of 1877 "A most liberal provision" — enabling the people of a district to vote upon the question of local tax to meet the cost of a longer term, it could hardly have been assessed as an act meeting the test of equality in the education of the two races. Negroes had been but a decade out of slavery and it would have been difficulty indeed for them to profit by this provision. This legislation failed to become a law for lack of the signatures of the heads of the Senate and of the House.

Scarborough's philosophy for an efficient school system was based upon his "Four Foundation Stones For Public Education" which would include the following:

A definite objective expressed in its curriculum

A complete organization by which it is to be reached

A body of efficient administrative officers for every department

Sufficient funds with which to finance the system successfully.

---

[2] *Biennial Report* 1876-77; Doc. 6, p. 17.

His organization would embrace the State Board of Education, the County Board of Education, the County Superintendent, and the teaching force.

The Legislature of 1881 abolished the office of County Examiner and authorized the appointment of a County Superintendent. The County Board of Education was created in 1885 for the function of administering the county school systems. It was to be elected by the Justices of the Peace and the County Commissioners. Its members were to be qualified by education and experience to "SPECIALLY" further the Public School interest.[3]

Fayetteville "Colored Normal"

The first of the Negro State Normal Schools, "The Colored Normal", was opened at Fayetteville in September 1877, authorized under the School Law adopted February 20, 1877. Robert Harris was its first principal. Harris, son of free parents, was born in North Carolina but migrated to Ohio where he had the advantage of a good education, especially at Oberlin College where he received his college training. He returned to the State during Reconstruction and was one of the Negro leaders in the Convention of 1869 which framed the first school law of the Reconstruction era. He headed one of the first Negro schools, known as the Howard School in Fayetteville which Assistant State Superintendent J. W. Hood reported as "The Best in the State" (Chapter I, q.v.)

The following note was contained in Scarborough's report dated January 1, 1878:

> A large and commodius school building, seventy by thirty-five feet, two stories high and well adapted to the purpose of such a school has been secured by the Board of Education. Students can procure board at from $5.00 to $8.00 per month according to quality. Reduced rates of fare over Rail Road will be secured and announced in due time. Colored youth desiring to improve their education and to aid in the education of their own people, have here an opportunity of doing so, through the liberality of the General Assembly. It is very important for students to be present at the opening of school. The Board earnestly recommends all who can to attend this school and prepare themselves for usefulness among people of their own race. For further particulars address Robert Harris, Fayetteville. Signed, Z. B. Vance, Governor; J. C. Scarborough, State Superintendent.[4]

The Board of Managers were listed as: E. J. Lilly, W. C. Troy, and J. H. Myrover. The Colored Normal at Fayetteville opened Sep-

---

[3]Noble, *Op. Cit.*, p. 383.

[4]*Scarborough's Annual Report*, January 1, 1878, pp. 24 ff.

tember 3, 1877 with 40 candidates for admission who were accepted and signed pledges to teach for three years. Females were admitted on equal terms with males. The students were grouped into three classes as follows: Seniors who numbered 11; Middle Class, 26; and Junior Class, 21. There were two assistant teachers. The normal was held in the same building as the Howard School which was large enough to accommodate both organizations.

While most of the students were local, some came from other counties. Harris reported those from other counties rather deficient in the rudiments and he planned to organize a preparatory class for them. A literary society had been formed and a "practice school" set up.

In admitting females (the term, female, was in general use at the time), Harris was ahead of his time for women had not officially been admitted to the University. However, Harris defended his policy as follows:

> Presence of females has a refining influence on manners of males and their reciting together in the same classes creates lively interest and incites a spirit of healthy emulation. In deportment and scholarship the females have shown themselves in no wise inferior to the males and the school would be deprived of some of its brightest students and most promising teachers if females were not admitted.

Harris reported some students having withdrawn because of lack of money and he had petitioned the Peabody Fund to come to his assistance in aiding such students to remain in school. In his report the second year of the school he reported 98 students (55 males; 33 females). There had come to him a great demand for good teachers, but he was beset by political 'tricksters' who claimed the school was being run to train Democrat voters.

> I regret to state that enemies of the school have been actively at work ever since its organization, poisoning the minds of the colored people in various parts of the State against the school by asserting that it is a democrat school; that it was established by the dominant party for the purpose of educating colored democrats and that students are trained and sent out as democrat canvassers . . . some students have even been threatened and many have been prevented from coming to the school.[5]

Bishop J. W. Hood, who lived in Fayetteville and had been associated with Harris since the early days of Reconstruction, ably defended Harris in the operation of the school. He realized that Harris' efforts to train teachers was one of the principal answers to the needs of the times. Said he:

---

[5]*Ibid.*, 1879, p. 35.

Much has been said of the inadequacy of our school funds; and much, also in the disparagement of our school laws, but these are not the only, nor the greatest obstacles in our way. WHAT WE NEED IS A SUFFICIENT NUMBER OF GOOD TEACHERS. If we had a supply of earnest, competent teachers and if the money collected for school purposes were expended only in support of schools taught by such teachers, a vast amount of good might be done, even with our limited means . . . . I once visited a school with a reported average attendance of 60, but I found only 4 actually present and was informed that there had never been an average of more than 10. I have witnessed the infliction of unreasonable and unsuitable punishment on scholars by a drunken teacher. I have heard incorrect pronunciation taught and bad reading uncorrected in numbers of schools kept by illiterate teachers. Quite recently, I met a teacher almost beastly drunk and was told that it was no unusual sight in that county. No time should be lost in relieving our schools of the incubus of teachers of bad character and poor education . . . . The State has done a noble act in establishing the Colored Normal at Fayetteville, and it should have the hearty support and encouragement of all who desire the improvement and performance of our public schools.[6]

The course of study of the Colored Normal, listed below, suggests a very comprehensive view of elementary teachers preparation of the period.

Junior Class

Reading, Articulation, Spelling, Defining, Dictation, Phonetics, Elementary Grammar, Primary Geography, Mental and Written Arithmetic, Writing, Drawing, Rudiments of Music, Theory and Practice, and Making and Keeping A Register.

Middle Class

United States History, Advanced Geography, Practical Grammar, Orthography, and Etymology, Mental and Written Arithmetic, Composition, Penmanship, Map Drawing, Spelling, Vocal Music, School Management and Discipline, and Declamation.

Senior Class

Universal History, Physiology, Astronomy, Algebra, Bookkeeping, Grammar, Composition, Analysis, Arithmetic

---

[6] *Ibid.*, p. 37.

reviewed, Geography reviewed, Spelling, Dictation, Oratory, Manners and Morals.

Harris' first students are listed by classes. Perhaps some of these family names, if not the actual individuals, are remembered by residents of Fayetteville and Cumberland County to-day (1963).

Senior Class

A. J. Chestnutt, Jr., J. W. Williams, H. C. Tyson, John Bain, D. W. Bryant, George H. Williams, T. H. McNeill, Hetty McNeill, Mary E. Leary, Jane E. Williams, Caroline Ingram, Mary J. Williams, Elizabeth H. Perry, Mary E. Pearce, D. W. Williams, W. H. McNeill.

Middle Class

John T. Williams, William Halsey, Alonzo Davis, W. E. Henderson, J. M. Hagler, P. M. Wyche, Jacob C. White, Frank Davis, Charles Cotten, J. B. Henderson, Rufus Collins, W. J. Cotten, Julia Ochiltree, Mary McCracken, Lina Pearce, Mary McLean, Ethel Leach, Charlotte Middleton, Carrie Perry, Rhoda Hogans, Georgiana Williams, Mary Scurlock, Elsie Stevens.

Junior Class, 1st Division

Sandy Stevens, George H. Evans, Thomas Williams, W. T. Tyson, W. B. Fenderson, Joseph C. White, Mary K. Thornton, Elizabeth Smith, Ann E. Hadley, Kate Bain, Susan Cain, Laura McDonald, David Hogans.

Junior Class, 2nd Division

Isaac Bain, C. M. McNeill, George H. Herring, Frank Hines, Thomas Chalmers, Alice Evans, Mary E. Moore, Martha Sammons, Louisa Council, Jennie Collins, Robert Wyche, J. A. Davis, O. E. Robinson, Joseph Millard, James Robinson, M. A. Cureton.

Junior Class, 3rd Division

C. C. Lomax, John Redick, Julia Maxwell, Annie C. Weddington, Nancy Moore (deceased), Lizzie Jones, Della Powell, L. A. Bennett, Anna Brown, Edward Evans, Sam Bogans, Ed Boykin, Moses Hines, H. S. Sellers, William L. Leary, Robert Kelley, Fannie Jackson, James Bryant, J. S. Gore, F. K. Fennell, Joseph Barge, P. O. Holmes, Charles McKay, J. C. McAllister.

Harris reported on his first closing exercises that the Junior Class gave a public exhibition consisting of essays and singing and that it was pronounced excellent by white and colored. The Senior and Middle Classes also held fitting exercises. The valedictory was given by H. C. Tyson of Carthage, Moore County. The Literary Society closed with a debate — Resolved that the Condition of the Colored people would be improved by emigration. It was well debated and was won by the negative. Signed Robert Harris, May 30, 1879.

The career of Robert Harris came to an end on October 24, 1880, at age of 41. On the occasion of his passing, Scarborough recorded in his report:

> He was a good man and true. He had excellent teaching capacity, a good mind, well stored with useful information, and was well trained in normal school work and was possessed of fine executive ability. The State Board was very largely indebted to him for the well nurtured plan of organization which has thus far brought very gratifying success to the operation of the school. His death is a public calamity and his place can not easily be filled.[7]

Charles W. Chestnut was appointed to head the Colored Normal upon the death of Robert Harris. It would seem appropos to note here the stature of the man who succeeded Robert Harris.

Born in Cleveland, Ohio, Chestnut had taught at Charlotte and later at Fayetteville as assistant to Harris. He wrote many volumes and also practiced law. As a novelist, Chestnut's reputation rests upon his pioneering in Race themes. He dared to mirror authentically: (1) the miseries of slavery; (2) the basic inter-racial and intra-racial problems of Reconstruction; and (3) discrimination, segregation, and miscegenation as prime factors in the race problems since Reconstruction. For his pioneering as such, he was awarded the Spingarn Medal in 1928.[8]

Four Additional Normal Schools

By the provisions of Section 5, Chapter 141, Laws of 1881, the State Board of Education established four additional normal schools at the following places: New Bern, Plymouth, Franklinton, and at Salisbury. The larger population of Colored people in the eastern counties determined the location of three of these in the East. Quoting Superintendent Scarborough:

> I thought it best, the State Board concurring, that the colored normals should continue for as long terms as funds appropriated would provide, believing that Colored teachers needed, more largely than whites, more instruction in the subject-matter to be learned from text-books than in method

---

[7]*Biennial Report* 1879-80; p. 37.

[8]N. C. Authors Handbook: Joint Committee N. C. English Teachers Association and N. C. Library Association, p. 21.

... this caused the schools to be organized on a plan for four of five months-session and combined drill and public school studies with methods of teaching, school organization, and government. . . Teachers prepared for work in these schools show very great improvement in character, matter, and method; and are far superior to the large number of Colored teachers whose education is defective.[9]

New Bern Normal was opened in July 1881 with G. H. White as Principal and with an enrollment of 63. At the start he was the sole teacher, but later was joined by two assistants, Miss Nancy Scott of Columbia, S. C. and William J. Heritage of Washington, D. C.*

Franklinton Normal was opened September 19, 1881, with an enrollment of 67 and with M. A. Hopkins as its Principal.

Salisbury Normal was opened August 17, 1881, with J. O. Crosby as Principal. His opening statement contained the following words:

> This school supplies a long-felt want. There is a great demand for teachers. A large per cent of teachers are 'third grade'; a few are 'special thirds'; and there are hundreds of schools without teachers of any grade.

Plymouth Normal was opened August 8, 1881, under the principalship of A. Hicks, Jr. His assistant and preceptress was Miss Leonora T. Jackson, who was prominent in normal school work at Fayetteville in the late 1920's.

Of these additional normal schools, Historian Noble wrote:
> These additional normal schools could do but little for training of the great number of teachers needed. Their advanced classes did practically the same work done in the 6th grade of the public schools of the same towns and cities. Many of their students went out teaching whether completing the course or not. To train a sufficient number of competent teachers to teach 235,911 colored children was a great undertaking whether in State normals, church, or private schools. In fact it was difficult to find students able to attend normals even though the tuition was free. Colored people were very poor. A farm hand made $8 or $9 a month and rations. Salaries of teachers were not an attraction. However, the establishment of the normals was a beginning of what ought to be. They are not equal (1930) to the needs, but have improved and will continue to send to colored schools every year increasing numbers of teachers of character, education, and devotion to their calling.[10]

---

[10]Noble, *Op. Cit.*, 426.

* (The name of P. W. Moore, later to become head of Elizabeth City State Normal, was listed as one of the first students.)

[9]*Biennial Report* 1881-82, p. 14 ff.

Scarborough's Report for 1882-84 lists the following early teachers in some of these Normals. H. C. Tyson, who was graduated Valedictorian under Harris at Fayetteville, and Miss Mary Leary were assistants at Fayetteville Normal. New Bern had William J. Heritage, Miss Nancy White, and W. H. Moore, who was a pupil, but taught one or more classes and was given a certificate. Salisbury had a Professor Richardson and Reverend F. C. Potter, who later resigned, and C. H. Moore, who succeeded Reverend Mr. Potter. Franklinton had Moses Hopkins as Principal and two assistants (names not known). However, under the direction of Hopkins, Reverend J. A. Savage, who later headed the Franklinton school, together with a Miss Ella Somerville of Washington, D. C. conducted a five weeks' course for teachers at New Bern in 1883.[11]

County Superintendent

The early recommendation for the establishment of a system of County Superintendents was made by Alexander McIver, in the 1870's, but it was not until 1881 that the Legislature finally listened well enough to provide for the office in place of the out moded County Examiner. The same Legislature provided for setting up county institutes for the improvement of teachers. These institutes were to be conducted by the Superintendent and all teachers were required to attend them. Under this new set-up many counties were redistricted with reference to proper size. The more people saw of an energetic superintendent, the more interested they became in the schools. Institutes were held in 58 counties in 1881-82 with 2,200 white and 650 colored teachers attending. Schools greatly improved under county supervision, both in the work of the teacher and in the advancement of the pupils.[12]

The Legislature of 1883 took a backward step in education when it curtailed the prestige of the County Superintendents by reducing their salary not to exceed 3% of the school funds instead of 5%. However, the Legislature of 1885 restored it, but required superintendents to be experienced teachers. It also created the County Board of Education and required it to prepare an estimate of the financial needs of education each year. The salary of the Clerk for the State Superintendent was increased from $600 to $1,000 and travel allowance from $500 to $750. Governor Jarvis recommended an increase in the salary of the State Superintendent.[13]

---

[11]*Biennial Report* 1882-84, p. 146.

[12]*Biennial Report* 1881-82, p. 21.

[13]Noble, *Op. Cit.*, p. 391.

Statistics at Close of Scarborough's Administration

Statistics for 1884 showed the following number of children:[14]

Number of white males 163,081; females, 151,212; total 314,293
Number of colored males 99,710; females, 90,278; total 189,988
Average attending:

> White male 91,044; white females 76,015; total 167,059
> Colored males 54,606; colored females 56,633; total 111,239
> Average monthly salary, white teachers, $24.16; colored $22.06.

During the Period, 1877-85, the more prominent leaders in all that was done for the public schools were Governors Vance and Jarvis and Superintendent John C. Scarborough. Vance worked for the training of both races; the whites at the University; the colored at Fayetteville. He visited both places while school was in session and insisted upon ample appropriation for both.

> While one system may be better than another, the most perfect is not worth the paper on which it is written without money to build school houses and pay teachers. . . . I beg that you will not forget to provide the money. This can be done by taxation. . . The tax is now only 8 and 1/3c on the $100.00 valuation and 25c on polls. Three times this would not be burdensome, but wise legislation.[15]

Despite his high standard of educational statesmanship, Scarborough failed of reelection in 1884, but destiny provided for him another term later as he succeeded Finger in 1893 for another term as State Superintendent.

------

[14]*Biennial Report* 1882-84, p. 199.

[15]Noble, *Op. Cit.*, p. 395.

Chapter IV

Administration Of Sidney M. Finger
1885-93

State Superintendent S. M. Finger was perhaps the first State Superintendent to recognize the importance of industrialization as an objective in public school education. The implication here is important in the light of a trend of the 1960's and of the later emphasis in this work on "Quality Education." It might be said that Finger early saw what many Twentieth Century educators have been slow to recognize.

To resurrect the age-old controversy which existed during the Booker T. Washington era between him and those who opposed his theory of industrial education is to get ahead of our story, but it is coincidental that Washington started his theory of education about the time that Finger was advocating practical training in the public schools of North Carolina. A full discussion of industrialization with respect to education will be made in a later chapter.

Finger, in the introduction of his Biennial Report, 1887-88 wrote as follows:

> Education is not merely or perhaps principally book learning — not merely a knowledge of Reading, Writing, Arithmetic, etc., which the boy and girl may carry into every day work, but education is development of brain power — a development of all the faculties of mind along with the physical powers and knowledge of facts. Our young people must be taught to think, reason, and observe for themselves, and any process that secures this result will educate them. Because manual labor is so great an educational factor and because children in the cities have not so great opportunities in this direction as do children of the rural, manual training for children of the cities in some substantial way . . . is a thing much to be desired. Besides, in this age of invention, a large proportion of work . . . is done by machinery. Consequently apprenticeship in mechanized trades has almost disappeared and skilled and well-trained workmen are becoming scarce. The education, therefore, needed in this direction is such training of the hand in the use of tools as will enable our people quickly to become expert in any kind of work which may be open to them.

As to rural education, Finger said that since three-fourths of the people were agriculturists, the 'country' schools should include in branches, not chemistry, but some text-book outlining the great elementary principles of agriculture.[1]

Education in the 80's

In the 1880's there was some reduction in illiteracy, especially among Negroes. Prior to 1900 the State had dismally failed to live up to the educational provisions of the Constitution and the law. In that year its public school system was actually and relatively worse than it had been in 1860. It was perhaps the poorest in the United States. Yet only 19.5 per cent of its white and 47.6 per cent of its Negroes were illiterate.

Public education in North Carolina was severely handicapped by relative poverty due to low income, scattered population, and bad roads. In addition there was the necessity of maintaining a dual system of schools. The standard explanations for educational backwardness were: the Negro, with fear of mixed schools, and poverty resulting from the Civil War. In reality there was no danger of mixed schools either from local demand or outside compulsion. The real reasons were colossal indifference to education and a sterile reactionary leadership which failed to press vigorously enough for educational improvement. Legislatures were indifferent; Governors, except Vance and Jarvis, made excuses, and local management was generally bad.[2]

Finger and Legislation

Prior to Finger's administration, the Legislature of 1880 had authorized the County of Wayne, if deemed necessary, to order an election in Goldsboro to determine whether a special tax of 1/5 of 1% on property and 60c on polls should be levied for graded schools; the tax to be collected from whites to be applied to white schools; that from colored to be applied to colored schools. No vote, however, was ever held under this act, but under an act of the Legislature March 5, 1881, an election was held on the question of levying in Goldsboro Township a special tax of 20c on property and 60c on polls for the support of graded schools; the tax to be apportioned by race.

Both races in Goldsboro Township voted in favor of the tax and the Goldsboro Graded Schools were opened in September 1881. Durham passed a similar act in 1882 and more graded school activity brought on the Dortch Bill (sponsor, W. T. Dortch, of Wayne) which provided that upon the petition of 10 white and 10 colored voters in any school district, the county commissioners should call an election for a special tax to be applied to the benefit of the race that voted it.

---

[1]Biennial Report 1887-88; Introduction, p. XXIX.

[2] Lefler and Newsome, *Op. Cit.*, p. 503.

Complications involving the division of the tax by race brought suits in Durham and in Gaston County. The N. C. Supreme Court declared the law unconstitutional — that taxes could not be apportioned on the basis of race. It was pointed out that Greensboro had established graded schools in 1870 which permitted no distinction between the races in the division of funds.[3]

The question of division of funds by race, however, continued to stalk the State's leadership even down to the time of Aycock in the early 1900's. Commenting upon the issue and the impact of the Court's decision, Superintendent Finger wrote at length:

> I find that quite a number of graded schools affected by the decision have already been discontinued while others have been sustained by private donations.[4]

While some towns wholly abolished plans for graded schools or closed those already established, others continued them with private contribution and all eventually sought legislation in conformity with the Supreme Court ruling. A few others voted a special tax to be divided without discrimination as to race.[5]

Of the Court's decision, Finger had the following to say:

> I am led by this declaration to suppose that any amendment to Graded School laws which would contemplate an equality of length of school terms for both races would be sustained by the Court. Indeed, I think it is well settled law, that public school money may be applied per capita upon school census, per capita upon average daily attendance, or in any other way so that equality of school facilities may be afforded.[6]

One of the most serious of the inequalities of public school education was the difference in length of terms in the rural and in the urban schools. The average length of terms in rural schools was about 13 weeks. Only cities and towns could vote the special tax providing for longer terms. These schools ran from 8 to 10 months. Only a blind leadership could fail to recognize the incongruity of such a condition.

Among those schools with special charters enabling them to conduct long term schools were: Murphy, Asheville, Salisbury, Shelby, Statesville, Concord, Charlotte, Greensboro, Winston, Wilson, Reidsville, Durham, Raleigh, Goldsboro and Tarboro. The cities of Wilmington and Fayetteville operated without special tax.*

---

[3] Noble, *Op. Cit.*, p. 404 ff.

[4] Major Finger's Report, 1885; p. 9.

[5] Noble, *Op. Cit.*, p. 408.

[6] Biennial Report 1891-92; p. 2.

* (An incomplete dated document, SPI files, State Archieves lists, Goldsboro Colored Graded School 1881, C. Dillard, Principal).

Private Schools

North Carolina owed a great debt to the long list of private schools, white and colored, which absorbed some of the slack caused by the poor leadership of which Lefler and Newsome (q.v.) spoke. While the free public schools were enduring periods of frustration, private schools had sprung up all over the State. Although occasional reports of the status of these private schools reached the State Superintendent, their statistics are not included in the official tabulations of enrollment and average daily attendance. Those colored private schools which did report to the State Superintendent are listed as follows:[7]

BIENNIAL, 1887-88

Beaufort County, Washington, L. R. Randolph Principal	35 pupils
Bertie County, Windsor, Emma Ward	20 pupils
Bertie County, Windsor, A. B. Cooper	10 pupils
Buncombe County, Asheville, Reverend Massiah	78 pupils
Cabarrus County, Concord-Scotia Seminary, Reverend D. J. Satterfield	195 pupils
Davie County, Mocksville, Mrs. Sophia B. Crawford	60 pupils
Edgecombe County, Coakley, Reverend R. Lawrance	268 pupils
Edgecombe County, Tarboro, Reverend J. W. Perry	92 pupils
Granville County, Oxford, M. C. Ransome	120 pupils
Hertford County, Winton, Reverend C. S. Brown	98 pupils
Mecklenburg County, Charlotte, Biddle University, Reverend S. Matoon	250 pupils
Rutherford County, Rutherfordton, Ellen Dade	105 pupils
Sampson County, Clinton, Normal Institute, G. H. Herring	55 pupils
Wake County, Raleigh, Shaw Universiy, Reverend Henry Martin Tupper	250 pupils
Warren County, Warrenton, Whitehead	180 pupils

Listed in Biennial Report, 1889-90

Bertie County, Windsor, Ranking, Richards Institute Rhoden Mitchell	154 pupils
Brunswick County, Southport, J. J. Clemons	30 pupils
Buncombe County, Episcopal Asheville, Reverend S. McDuffy	60 pupils
Buncombe County, Asheville, College St. School, Miss F. V. Russell	220 pupils
Buncombe County, Asheville, Sheppard Academy, Miss N. Leatherwood	61 pupils
Beaufort County, Washburn Seminary, H. W. Lewis	53 pupils

---

[7] Biennial Report 1887-88; p. 130.

Chatham County ....- Griffin   25 pupils
Cumberland County ...., Mission School, H. C. Mabry 107 pupils
Chowan County, Edenton, C. M. Cartwright   81 pupils
Duplin Couny, Kenansville, Hiram Brown   21 pupils
Durham County, Woodards High School,
            W. T. H. Woodward   137 pupils
Gaston County, Lincoln Academy, Miss E. C. Pruden   113 pupils
Granville County, Oxford, Reverend M. C. Ransom   200 pupils
Granville County, Buchram, S. S. Henderson   200 pupils
Granville County, Oxford, Reverend G. C. Shaw   30 pupils
Granville County, Adoniram, Reverend W. A. Patillo   38 pupils
Hyde County, Englehard   30 pupils
Guilford County, Greensboro, Bennett Seminary,
            Prof. C. N. Grandison   171 pupils
Guilford County, McLeansville, Bethany High School,
            Reverend Alfred Connet   48 pupils
Macon County, Franklin, J. T. Kennedy   54 pupils
Montgomery County, Troy, Peabody Institute,
            Miss Bessie C. Becham   69 pupils
Montgomery County, Dry Creek, K. J. Powell   40 pupils
Moore County, Carthage, Reverend H. D. Wood   115 pupils
New Hanover County, Wilmington, Charles T. Coerr   133 pupils
New Hanover County, Wilmington, Gregory Institute,
            George A. Woodard   352 pupils
New Hanover County, Wilmington Academy of
            Incarnation, Sister Mary Baptist   150 pupils
New Hanover County, Wilmington, Independent,
            Reverend L. T. Christmas   49 pupils
Northampton County, Garysburg, Garysburg High
            School, R. J. Walden   35 pupils
Pasquotank County, Elizabeth City, George A. Mebane 63 pupils
Pender County, Long Creek, Long Creek Normal,
            Professor Jacobs   43 pupils
Pender County, Burgaw, Burgaw Normal, Wesley Jones   30 pupils
Person County, Roxboro, C. H. Hester   65 pupils
Pitt County, Greenville, Sam Humphrey   70 pupils
Pitt County, Greenville, Humphrey Institute, W. J. Solomon 40 pupils
Vance County, Kittrell, Kittrell Normal, John R. Hawkins 140 pupils
Warren County, Warrenton High School, J. A. Whitted 93 pupils

Biennial Report 1891-92

Brunswick County, Southport, Mamie Griffin   21 pupils
Brunswick County, Southport, L. J. Spells   12 pupils
Brunswick County, Southport, Academy, J. J. Clemons 47 pupils
Carteret County, Washburn Academy, Miss M. E. Wilcox 64 pupils
Chowan County, Edenton, Mattie Mebane   6 pupils
Chowan County, Edenton, Mrs. V. Barclay   11 pupils
Chowan County, Edenton, Mrs. H. Bedham   41 pupils

Chowan County, Edenton, N. E. Jones   30 pupils
Dare County, Roanoke, California, John W. Barrington   40 pupils
Edgecombe County, Tarboro, Perry Academy,
          Reverend Perry   109 pupils
Johnston County, Smithfield, Smithfield Preparatory,
          John W. Byrd   60 pupils
Johnston County, Selma, Selma Academy, R. L. Atkinson 38 pupils
Johnston County, Clayton, Clayton Prep., L. C. Mial   64 pupils
Richmond County, Rockingham, Reverend Myer   60 pupils
Robeson County, Lumberton, Whiten Normal, David P. Allen
Washington County

Normal Schools

The State supported normal schools were by far the most important asset of the State in its effort to educate colored children for they
supplied most of the best teachers. However, the work of the private
schools can in no wise be minimized for out of them came the foremost
leaders of the race. Especially is this true of Shaw University, Biddle
(Johnson C. Smith), Saint Augustine's College and Livingstone College.

Of the normal schools Finger said that while they had been successful in training many teachers, they needed more money to accomplish their objectives. There were five of these State normals
under Finger's administration and many legislators felt that the
number should be reduced and the appropriation increased. Fayetteville, the first to be established (1877) had an annual appropriation
of $2,000; the additional four, $500 each. By the Laws of 1887, Chapter 408, the annual appropriation for the four additional normals was
increased to $6,000, making the total annual appropriation $8,000
for the five colored normals.[8]

Franklinton State Normal, established in 1881, was reported in
the 1884-85 Biennial as having run for 7 months each year and had
enrolled 430 pupils coming from 29 different counties. Moses Hopkins
was the first principal and had two assistants. Names of his first
pupils have familiar names, some of which might be remembered by
citizens of Franklin County. A few are listed:

W. H. Dunston, William Dunston, Robert Cannady, Sarah
Perry, J. P. Person, Sallie Person, Roberta Dunston, Charlie
Person, J. M. Hawkins, Addie McGowan, Jeff D. Yarboro,
William S. King, Elbert B. Alston, J. C. Hawkins, Robert
Dunston, William R. Slade.[9]

Many of his students became active teachers in this state and in
Virginia. Hopkins went to Africa in 1885 and S. A. Waugh became

---

[8] *Ibid.*, p. 67.

[9] Biennial Report 1883-84; p. 92.

principal. His assistants were Miss Mary Lettson and John N. Conyard. In 1891 by Act of the Legislature, the school was moved to Warrenton with J. A. Whitted as principal.[10]

Plymouth Normal

A. B. Hicks, Jr., a brilliant young man who held a college degree, was the first principal of the Plymouth Normal. He died while in office at the age of twenty-seven and was succeeded by H. P. Cheatham.* Upon the death of Hicks, Cheatham said:

> The school and the State have lost one of its best instructors and an excellent citizen. He stood well as a man of unquestionable character among people of both races of his section. He had represented Washington County in the Legislature of 1881 and at the time of his death was a member of the Board of County Commissioners of Washington County, elected by Democrats.

Cheatham's salary was $50.00 per month and that of his two assistants, $40.00 each. Instrumental music was taught by Mrs. L. S. Cheatham. Some of the names listed on his student roll were: Aaron B. Cooper, Bertie; Moses W. Norman, Washington; L. L. Boyd, Elizabeth City; J. S. Sessom, Hertford; W. C. Wynn, Halifax; J. J. Hoggard, Edenton; C. G. White, Bethel; Willie Ann Hyman, Plymouth and W. H. Riddick, Plymouth.[11]

Cheatham resigned in 1884 and was succeeded by John W. Pope. The high esteem in which Cheatham was held is evidenced in a letter from Reverend F. A. Bishop, pastor of the M. E. Church (South) written to Superintendent Scarborough in which he said:

> He is thorough in his methods and earnestly endeavors to have his pupils clearly understand everything so they can tell it to others.[12]

Pope's assistants were T. S. Davis and Emma Timberlake. He wrote to Superintendent Finger that the building was unfit for a school; that it was badly in need of repairs and that he had to cut off one assistant because of lack of funds.[13]

H. C. Crosby succeeded Pope and wrote Finger that a new building to accommodate the Normal was being constructed. He enrolled

---

[10] Biennial Report 1891-92; p. 50.

* Cheatham later served in Congress, 1889-93, and still later headed the Colored Orphanage at Oxford.

[11] Biennial Report 1883-84; p. 98 ff.

[12] Superintendents Correspondence; Letter to J. C. Scarborough; Letter Box 146.

[13] Biennial Report 1885-86; p. 72.

64 students in 1887 and by 1891-92 he had enrolled 119. His assistants were J. W. McDonald, P. W. Moore, and Miss E. J. Timberlake.[14]

New Bern Normal

A special summer session was held at the New Bern State Normal in August of 1883 under the supervision of a Miss Ella Somerville of Washington, D. C. and under the direction of the Reverend M. A. Hopkins, the Reverend J. A. Savage, and L. T. Christmas. The school enrolled 116 teachers. Among the instructors were: Miss Marian P. Shadd, in charge of Algebra, oral arithmetic, history, and physiology; Miss Mamie E. Nichols, teacher of calisthenics, music, and drawing; and Miss Rosetta E. Coakley, teacher of geography, map drawing, penmanship, reading, and spelling. These instructors came from Washington, D. C. and vicinity. Miss Somerville taught written arithmetic, grammar, physics, and pedagogics.

Some of the names listed in the report are: George Dudley, Sarah Dudley, Mary Franks, Alexander Moore, David Mosely, Sarah E. McDaniel, Emma Sutton, all of New Bern; Roxana Shepherd, of Goldsboro; George W. Smith of Hyde County; Mary Smallwood of New Bern and Louisa Nixon of Wilmington. Miss Somerville was paid a total of $332 for her work and that of her teachers.[15]

Salisbury Normal

J. O. Crosby, Principal at the Salisury Normal, had as his assistant, Prof. C. H. Moore, who, in later years was quite a leading educator. The meagre equipment of the Salisbury Normal included two good sets of apparatus — philosophical and arithmetical and a choice library of 300 volumes donated by northern friends. Nearly all the text books were given to the school, but the crying need, like the other normals, was funds to carry on the work.

Some of Crosby's early students were: C. C. Somerville, Warren; A. A. Wood, Franklin; Mary Hargrave, Salisbury; E. G. Montgomery, Concord; Daisy Kirkpatrick, Greensboro; C. W. Boyd, Salisbury; Alice McConnaughey, Rowan; G. W. Alston, Concord; H. Correll, Salisbury; Thomas Long and George Long, Salisbury; H. H. Hall, David Hall, and James McCorkle, of Salisbury.[16]

Crosby's third session began September 3, 1883, during which he enrolled 105 students. Thirty-five of his previous students were engaged in teaching in various counties. The term started out with three assistants, but one was released because of lack of funds to pay salaries. Special attention was given to essay writing, School Organ-

---

[14] Biennial Report 1891-92.

[15] Biennial Report 1883-84; p. 94.

[16] *Ibid.*, p. 91.

ization and Discipline, Method of Instruction, Culture and School Law.[17]

There were three graduates of Crosby's fourth session. They were: C. C. Somerville of Warrenton, Miss H. Stanard of Salisbury, and P. N. Melchoir of Concord. The enrollment was 134. Some 10 or 12 students taught one or more classes in the Graded School which was under the supervision of the Normal. Crosby's teachers were listed as follows: C. A. Isbel, G. W. Austin, A. A. Carson, M. L. Young, Miss Cora Goodwyn, and Miss Fannie Clements.[18]

Goldsboro Normal

On January 6, 1881, C. B. Aycock wrote to Superintendent J. C. Scarborough requesting the location of a normal school in Goldsboro. He stated that the County of Wayne would give $200 toward expenses and that more could be raised if necessary. The urgency of his request was expressed as follows:

> We need it "bad"; every teacher in the county is anxious for it.[19]

The General Assembly at its 1885 session directed the Normal School at New Bern to be moved to Goldsboro. On February 15, 1886, an announcement by the Trustees of the Goldsboro Graded Colored School stated that an organization of a normal and classical institute had been effected in connection with the regular course of study adopted for that school. This announcement was signed by C. N. Hunter, Superintendent, Goldsboro Colored Graded School, J. A. Bonitz, Editor *Goldsboro Messenger,* and E. A. Wright, Wayne County Superintendent of Schools.

On October 12, 1887, E. A. Alderman, Superintendent of Goldsboro Schools, wrote Superintendent Finger that the Normal Board had elected W. T. Kornegay, Chairman and Major Grant, Secretary-Treasurer; that a building was nearing completion and that a principal was soon to be selected.[20]

L. P. Perry was the first principal. In 1889-90 the principal was S. B. Pride who had as an assistant, Miss Louise S. Dorr, who had been credited with the establishing of the Goldsboro Normal and Classical Institute. It appears that the Goldsboro State Normal and the Goldsboro Normal and Classical Institute were the same institu-

---

[17] *Ibid.,* p. 190.

[18] Biennial Report 1885-86; p. 86.

[19] Superintendents Correspondence; Letter — Aycock to Supt. Scarborough; State Archives.

[20] *Ibid.,* Alderman to Finger; State Archives.

tion. A. L. Summer became principal in 1894 and had as assistants, Mary E. Fonveille and Polk Fonveille.*

A number of private schools attached the term, "normal" to their names and, although they had no official status, many of them were credited with boosting the educational program of the State in training teachers. For example, Whiten Normal at Lumberton, headed by David P. Allen was one such school. Years later while instructing in the summer school of Fayetteville State Normal, this author had the pleasure of knowing some of Whiten Normal's former students who showed superior training. A son of David P. Allen, George Leonard Allen (now deceased) once taught at Dillard High School in Goldsboro under the principalship of this author. Another son, Dr. D. P. Allen, Jr., is now a practicing physician in Charlotte (1963).

Elizabeth City State Normal

On January 20, 1883, a letter signed by several prominent citizens of Elizabeth City was received by Superintendent J. C. Scarborough. This letter recommended Rooks Turner as a highly capable graduate who had been operating a school in a building he had erected himself. His school ran for 8 months and was located in a region of large numbers of colored people. Among other things, the letter stated:

> Our people would be glad to see the educational interest of the colored people promoted by his advancement.

The letter obviously was meant to enhance the prospect of moving the normal school from Plymouth as considerable speculation relative to moving the school from Plymouth had been in the air. However, the General Assembly did not get around to establishing the normal at Elizabeth City until 1891 and it was H. C. Crosby, the Plymouth Normal head, who recommended the man to be the principal. It was P. W. Moore whose name has been enshrined in the hearts of thousands of students whose lives were influenced by his great soul.

Moore began his school on January 4, 1892, with J. H. Butler as his assistant and enrolled 69 students from nine different counties. The first term ran 20 weeks.[22]

A. and M. College (A. and T. College)

Another notable event of the Finger Administration was the establishment of the A. and M. College (now A. and T. College) which was originally set up as an annex to Shaw University at Raleigh with John O. Crosby as its first administrator.

It was moved to Greensboro in 1893 with James B. Dudley, A. M. of Livingstone College as its first president. The objective of the in-

---

* Mary E. Fonveille became the second wife of Reverend C. Dillard.

[22] Brown, A. History of Education of Negroes in North Carolina, p. 87.

P. W. MOORE, *Founder*
State Normal School
Elizabeth City State Teachers College

JAMES B. DUDLEY
President, A&T College, — 1896-1925

stitution was for the teaching of Agriculture, Mechanical Arts, and such branches of learning as relate thereto.

Aside from James B. Dudley, the faculty was composed as follows: C. H. Moore, A. M., Amherst College, English; John Thompson, B. Ag., University of Minnesota, Professor of Agriculture; Jesse Haskell Bourne, M. E., Massachusetts Institute of Technology, Professor of Mechanics and Mathematics; John H. M. Butler, A. M., Livingstone College, Principal Preparatory Department; Miss S. M. Parker, Saint Augustine's College, Domestic Science; D. A. Williston, B. S. A., Cornell University, Instructor in Agriculture; Miss M. R. Perry, High School, Washington, D. C., Instructor in Preparatory Department; C. H. Evans, Hampton Institute, Instructor in Wood-turning; S. G. Snow, Massachusetts Normal School, Agriculture and Drawing; R. W. Richardson, Instrumental Music; Miss A. V. Williams, Matron; and J. Rooks, Steward.

The curriculum comprised four departments: Agriculture, Mechanical, English, and Domestic Science. [23]

The Administration of Major S. M. Finger came to an end in 1893 when his predecessor, J. C. Scarborough (1877-85), was elected again to the position. In spite of wide spread opposition to taxation for schools and criticism of education in general, Finger adhered to his belief in publicly supported education. When he assumed office in 1885, 298,166 children out of 530,127 (six to twenty-one) were in attendance. At the close of his administration in 1893, there were 356,958 children out of a total of 618,541 (six to tweny-one) in attendance in the public schools. Seventy counties reported private schools of 8-months duration or more, with an enrollment of 25,110. An estimate of the number in the counties failing to report would make an approximate number of 30,000 children in private schools. The sad fact remained that about half the children were not in school at all. "If influential men would encourage them, many more would attend."[24]

On the question of taxation, Finger was quite realistic:

If you are opposed to taxation for public schools for any reason, look at your tax receipt and see how little you really pay on your property. . . . Can North Carolina afford to lag behind her sister southern states? We are much behind Virginia and Tennessee and all the southern states but one or two in length of term.

Perhaps you say, 'the Negroes are in the way', but do you know that, including the poll-tax, which they actually pay, and fines, forfeitures, and penalties, the Negroes furnish a

<hr>

[23] Biennial Report 1889-90; p. 56.

[24] Biennial Report 1885-86; General Rem., p. 2.

large proportion of the money that is applied to their public schools.[25]

---

[25] Biennial Report 1893-94; p.

Chapter V

Administration Of J. C. Scarborough
1893-1897

It will be remembered that Superintendent J. C. Scarborough was defeated for reelection in 1885 by Major S. M. Finger. It was a singular coincidence that in the same year president Grover Cleveland was defeated for re-election to the presidency of the United States; and four years later, both men defeated their successors in office.

It might appear incongruous that so important an office as the head of the school system should be motivated by the exigencies of politics when the future of children is involved. Yet the record of most of the State Superintendents seems to have shown a rather high degree of statesmanship in the men who have held this exalted position.

Scarborough entered upon the duties of his 'split' second administration with a recognition of the high standard which had been set by his predecessor, Major S. M. Finger. He immediately adopted the course of study which Finger initiated as a guide to public school teachers.

Concerning equal education, race-wise, very little had been said since early administrations, so long as there was no advocacy of mixed schools. The course of study, on its face, was the same for both races, but the discrepancies in facilities of the colored schools were appalling. Teachers' salaries, poor as they were for both races, were lower as a rule for colored teachers. It was even stated that because of a lower economic status the Negro teachers ought not have the same salaries as white teachers. A common complaint centered about the amount of taxes paid by Negroes in contrast with that paid by whites: that tax money should be divided according to the race paying it. However, the courts decreed that any division of the taxes on the basis of race was unconstitutional.

In the introduction of his first report, 1892-93, Scarborough urged teachers to strive earnestly to have pupils become interested in completing the steps year by year and to secure such cooperation by parents as would induce them to purchase for their children not only text-books, but other books to induce them to read. Such would give needed information and build vocabularies.[1]

The main problem of public school education continued to be the lack of enough money to operate the schools. In the school year of 1895-96 the total received for education was $824,238.08 which paid

---

[1]Biennial Report 1892-93, p. 31.

for a fraction less than 13 weeks or 63 school days. This was 17 days short of the Constitutional requirement of the 4-months school term for every county.

In 1895 the office of County Superintendent was abolished and its duties were placed in the hands of the Clerk of the County Board of Commissioners. The same act abolished the County Board of Education and turned their duties over to the County Commissioners. Provision was made for county examiners. The arrangement lasted two years when the County Board of Education was restored and provision made for a supervisor of schools with duties practically the same as superintendent.[2]

To meet the requirement of the Constitution for the 4-Months term, Scarborough said that the Legislature ought not stop short of 22¢ on the $100 valuation.

> Private schools don't meet the problem as they reach only about 7% of the children. . . . We must have the public schools, or our people are doomed to ignorance.

He vigorously recommended the restoration of the county superintendents and the county boards of education which had been abolished in 1895.

> It is impossible for county commissioners to administer the schools. No county board can do so without an executive officer. Nothing has been saved by abolishing county boards of education, county superintendents, and institutes.

He also recommended the continuation of the colored normals as they had been of immeasurable benefit to the country and village public schools for colored children by supplying teachers for them.[3]

Institute Work

With the establishing of the Normal and Industrial School at Greensboro for whites, the institutes or short term schools declined; particularly so as the $4,000 per annum appropriated in 1889 for institute work was now being applied to the support of the Normal and Industrial School. However, during the summer of 1893, seven hundred dollars was expended for institute work for both races in the Counties of Johnston, Pitt, Green, Wilson, Onslow, Jones, Robeson, and Richmond. These institutes were conducted by M. C. S. Noble of Wilmington and Alexander Graham of Charlotte. Much good was reported accomplished for both white and colored teachers.

The Peabody Fund had furnished money for the institute work, but withheld any further funds since the State did not appropriate

---

[2]Knight, *The Public School In North Carolina*, p. 320.

[3]Biennial Report 1894-96, p. 2 ff.

anything. The total attendance at these institutes of 1893 was 367 white and 555 colored teachers.

B. F. Blair, Superintendent of Greensboro, held an institute the same summer for colored teachers in the Colored Graded School, Number 2 in South Greensboro. The opening attendance was fairly good, but gradually increased to over 100 before the end of the session. Fifteen counties were represented. Teachers manifested much interest to become more thorough and efficient. The course was described as follows:

> Imparting the best and most effective methods of teaching, and also real class-work in various branches, including sounds of letters, spelling, reading, geography, grammar, arithmetic, physical geography, physiology, history, and political economy.

The teaching force consisted of 2 white and 2 colored instructors.[4]

McIver and Alderman

Charles D. McIver and Edwin A. Alderman, two young teachers, began to attract attention, not only in North Carolina, but in other states by their zeal and interest in behalf of "Universal Education." They were, like John, the Baptist, "Voices crying in the wilderness"; preparing the way for a greater than they, viz., Charles B. Aycock, who was later to become the epitome of Universal Education.

McIver and Alderman pleaded with legislators for more effecient facilities. They conducted institutes, canvassed the State, held educational meetings to enlist the interest of all the people for more and better education for all the children of both races. For two years they went up and down the State preaching the gospel of Universal Education. They succeeded in converting the Farmers Alliance, an organization of power and influence in the State. The Legislature of 1891, largely controlled by this organization, established the State Normal and Industrial College for white and the A. and M. College for colored, both at Greensboro.[5]

Peabody Contributions

The Peabody Fund, which had earlier contributed to the encouragement of many small schools, relinquished its policy in favor of giving scholarships to white teachers at certain outstanding institutions and contributions to the colored normals and some of the well established graded schools. While the amounts often seemed too small to accomplish much good, they did serve to encourage local

---

[4]Biennial Report 1892-94, pp. 43, 46.

[5]Knight, Op. Cit., p. 322.

initiative and it must be remembered that the Peabody Fund was stretched over the entire South in its objective to help impoverished communities recover from the effects of the Civil War. The following list of institutions helped in 1895 is but a sample of many grants made by the Fund:

Goldsboro Normal, H. L. Grant, Treasurer $100
Salisbury Normal, J. Rumple, Treasurer 100
Franklinton Normal, B. W. Ballard, Treasurer 100
Plymouth Normal, J. F. Norman, Treasurer 100
Elizabeth City, F. F. Cohoon, Treasurer 600

Grants made in February, 1896:

Fayetteville Normal, A. H. Slocumb, Treasurer $250
Durham Graded (colored), C. W. Toombs,
    Treasurer 200
Salisbury Normal 230
Franklinton Normal 230
Goldsboro Normal 230
Plymouth Normal 230
Elizabeth City 660
Slater Normal (Winston) 370

Grants made in May of 1896:

Fayetteville Normal .... $ 40
Franklinton 60
Goldsboro 60
Plymouth 60
Elizabeth City 130
Slater Normal 90

The Normal and Industrial College for white females at Greensboro was promised $2,800, of which $500 had already been paid. Further amounts promised to colored normals by the Fund included: Fayetteville $190, Franklinton $290, Goldsboro $290, Plymouth $290, and Elizabeth City $790.

The Normal Department of Slater Industrial Academy at Winston was established by Act of the Legislature in 1895. It was promised a sum of $460. The Manual Training Department of Durham Public School was promised $300 for the 1895 term.

"All These funds are handled through the State Superintendent as he thinks best."

J. L. M. Curry, Agent
PEABODY FUND[6]

---

[6]Biennial Report 1894-96, p. Grants to Normal Schools.

Reports of Normal Schools

Fayetteville — The Sixteenth Annual Session opened September 5, 1892, and closed May 19, 1893. There were enrolled 130 students representing 11 counties. There were 4 graduates. The report stated that since the establishment of the institution, 760 had enrolled from 66 different counties and that 117 had completed the course. During the term of 1893-94, there were 106 enrolled with an average attendance of 90; five completed the course and of these 4 took the teachers examination and received First Grade certificates. G. H. Williams was principal at the time. William's assistants in 1891 were listed as J. F. K. Simpson and Miss Libbie Leary.[7]

The session of 1895-96 enrolled 154 students. An additional year was added to the course during this session; hence there were no grad-uates. Visitors listed during the year included; The Honorable J. C. Scarborough, D. J. Sanders of Biddle University, Bishop J. W. Hood, and Professor C. Dillard of Goldsboro Graded Schools. The last two weeks of the term were devoted to institute work at which 115 were enrolled. E. E. Smith had returned as Principal.[8] (E. E. Smith had served as U. S. Minister to Liberia.)

Goldsboro Normal

The session of 1892-93 enrolled 128 students representing 12 different counties. There was one graduate. The report stated that the interest manifested by Goldsboro citizens was good. An industrial department had been organized. The report listed assistants as: Mrs. A. L. Dillard, Miss L. S. Dorr and Mrs. Julia B. Hagans. (Mrs. Julia B. Hagans was domestic arts teacher in the "Colored High School" (Dillard High) in Goldsboro in 1924 when the author assumed the principalship. The principal of Goldsboro Normal is 1892-93 was H. E. Hagans).

The session of 1893-94 ran for 10 months including a one-month's institute. The entire enrollment was 149. There were no graduates in 1894. The report stated that deportment was good, public interest was growing, and a manual department had been organized. S. G. Atkins, of the Slater Normal, assisted with the institute. The regular assistants were Miss L. S. Door and Mrs. G. T. Wassom. The institute enrolled 57 from Wayne and adjoining counties. R. S. Rives was the principal.[9]

Plymouth Normal

The session, 1892-93 enrolled 140 students representing 19 counties. The assistants were John W. McDonald and Miss Emma J.

---

[7] Biennial Report 1892-94, p. 61.

[8] Biennial Report 1894-96, p. 66.

[9] Biennial Report 1892-94, p. 66.

E. E. SMITH
Long time Principal of Fayetteville State Normal

S. G. ATKINS
*Founder of Slater Normal — Merged into Winston-Salem
State Normal*

Dance. The 1893-94 session enrolled 161 students representing 19 counties. One student, Miss Mary M. Summer of Gates County, completed the course and received the diploma. The *Roanoke Times* for June 8, 1894, highly praised the school and its principal, H. C. Crosby.[10]

The 18th Annual session enrolled 184 students. There were three assistants listed as follows: Professor J. W. McDonald, Mrs. Emma Dance, and Professor R. R. Cartright. Crosby was firm believer in teaching thoroughness in subject matter before stressing method. He was opposed to the idea of combining the seven normals into three—a trend which was to reach fruition later.[11]

Elizabeth City Normal

The second annual session of the institution, 1892-93, showed 69 enrolled representing nine counties. In the second half of the term, the number had nearly doubled; 120 from 14 counties having enrolled. During the term 1893-94, the enrollment reached 173, representing 17 counties. There were three assistants in 1895: Miss C. N. Kornegay, Mrs. F. B. Norman, and J. W. Brown. P. W. Moore, who had been an assistant to H. C. Crosby at Plymouth was the principal. He had been highly recommended by former State Superintendent, Major S. M. Finger[12]

Salisbury Normal

The 12th annual session, 1892-93, enrolled 118 students from 14 different counties. Two were graduated. In 1893-94 there were six graduates. The school had 60 volumes in its library. Its main effort during the term was the endeavor to secure a permanent location for the school. The principal in 1894 was F. M. Martin. John O. Crosby was principal in 1895.[13]

Franklinton Normal

The colored Normal, which had been moved to Warrenton, was ordered by the Legislature of 1893 to be transferred back to Franklinton. The term, 1893-94, enrolled 215, representing 23 counties. Seven teachers were employed and prominent lecturers helped in the work. The Reverend John A. Savage, was the principal.[14]

---

[10]*Ibid.*, p. 69.

[11]Biennial Report 1894-96, p. 76.

[12]Brown, *Op. Cit.*, p. 87.

[13]Biennial Report 1892-94, p. 59.

[14]*Ibid.*, p. 77.

Slater Normal

The Legislature of 1895, under Chapter 393, Public Laws of 1895, ordered the establishment of a normal school at or near Winston or Salem to absorb the Slater Normal and Industrial School. It opened in the fall of 1895 with S. G. Atkins as principal. Atkins stated its objectives as a thorough grounding of the students pursuing normal courses in subjects which they will be teaching; and a thorough acquaintance with the underlining principles of the science and art of education. The faculty consisted of C. G. O'Kelly, Thomas R. Debnam, and H. H. Hall. S. G. Atkins, Principal.[15]

The annual appropriation for the colored normals from 1887 to 1895 had been $8,500. This was increased to $10,500 in 1895 and in 1897 was increased to $14,500. An additional note of educational progress was seen in the growth of the graded schools. During the years, 1887 to 1897, graded schools increased rapidly and by 1899, 27 towns had graded schools supported largely by local taxation.[16]

Statistics of the Scarborough Administration

In 1896, the school census showed 420,809 white and 223,376 colored children, six to twenty one, in the State. The enrollment for this year was 231,059 white and 117,551 colored children. The average daily attendance was 137,115 white; 67,088 colored. The average length of term, 12.42 weeks for whites and 11.75 for colored. The average monthly salary for white males, $24.75; females, $21.64. For colored teachers: male, $26.70; female, $20.96. The value of white school property was $654,925.75; colored $233,206.60.[17]

Looking back over the second administration of J. C. Scarborough, it is at once recognized that some progress in the sum total was made toward equality, imperceptible as it may have been. The status of the colored normals, with their appropriations almost doubled, represents a degree of progressive equality which cannot be overlooked. The growth of graded schools in the urban centers had its measure of benefits toward equality. The establishing of the Elizabeth City State Normal and the absorption of Slater Normal were acts of enduring statesmanship which have redounded to the welfare of Negroes to this day (1963).

On the darker side of the image of Scarborough's administration is the inglorious fact that nearly half the State's children still were not attending school at all and the inequality of the school terms between rural and urban systems remained a sad commentary on the school system as a whole. The rural child by law could hope for only

---

[15]Biennial Report 1894-96, p. 89.

[16]Knight, *Op. Cit.*, p. 322.

[17]Biennial Report 1894-96, pp. 45, 52.

four months, while his city cousin could get eight to ten months of education.

Then there was the vacillation of different legislatures. The Legislature of one year moved Franklinton Normal to Warrenton; the next Legislature ordered it returned. One legislature abolished the County Board of Education and the Office of County Superintendent a later one restored them. The net results of these activities gave to J. C. Scarborough an honored place in the State's record of educational endeavor.

Chapter VI

Administration Of Charles H. Mebane
1897-1900

At this point, mid-way of our story of Equal and Quality Education, the reader might begin to wonder if the writer is on his subject. Indeed it may be necessary at times for the reader to look between the lines in order to observe any approach to the subject. Progress toward equality can only be shown through citing the historical facts which indicate the progressive movement toward equality. As for the other side of the subject, Quality Education, it must be left for the later chapters; yet a careful perusal of the activities of the era covered in the first half of the story would indicate a high degree of Quality Education shown by the leaders. When we consider the educational programs of the institutes, normal schools, summer schools, and the professional organizations, it would be difficult to deny the assertion that public school teachers were laying a sure foundation upon which Quality Education would be erected.

In Chapter V, we mentioned the possible impact of politics upon education. State Superintendent Mebane, although a product of political maneuvering, turned his back upon politics which, too long, had influenced legislation for schools. Mebane went straight to the people. Like Wiley, he used the newspapers effectively and was able to induce the FUSION LEGISLATURE to pass the most advanced law for local taxation yet proposed.

It directed that an election on the question of local taxation be held in every school district and, if defeated at the first election, another was to be held every two years until the law was finally passed.

Although this provision helped to educate the people on the subject of Education, it was very untimely, for the people were not prepared for such advanced action and only a dozen districts voted the tax.[1]

In the introductory statements of his first Biennial Report, Mebane stated that his purpose was to secure information pertaining to rural schools, city schools, private academies, and colleges. He wanted the best qualified men to administer the schools, politics notwithstanding:

We haven't had the best qualified men to fill the offices of county examiner, county superintendent, or county sup-

---

[1] Dabney, Charles William, *Universal Education in the South*, p. 214.

ervisor because of politics. The public schools have been in the galling grasp of the court house politicians for twenty years in some counties.[2]

Compulsory Attendance

Mebane was the first State Superintendent since McIver to advocate compulsory attendance. Noting, as the reader might well do also, that the statistics from administration to administration showed half the children (6 to 21) not even enrolled in the public schools and the attendance not much better than half the enrollment, Mebane said:

> I believe it right for the people to pay taxes for schools and that it is also right to force children to receive the benefit. North Carolina will have a compulsory attendance law some day. Why not now? Why stand we idle when thousands are growing up in ignorance?

In comparing attendance with illiteracy in 31 states, Mebane showed North Carolina, by the 1890 Census, with 36% illiteracy as against a low of from 3 to 14% in northern and western states. Of the strictly southern states, only Virginia, Arkansas, and Tennessee had a lower percentage than North Carolina. As for the white population alone, the State had a high percentage of 23, or more than any other southern state.

College heads, other educational leaders, and many of the newspapers of the State favored Mebane in his advocacy. *The Greensboro Telegram* published letters from numerous citizens in favor of legislation along this line.

Supervision

As for supervision, Mebane was equally insistent:

> We have road supervisors. We are not willing that earth and stones shall be handled without supervision. It will bring order and system out of confusion and chaos in many places where teachers are young and inexperienced. He (sic) will create interest where there is none and will infuse life and inspiration into schools which have become dry and monotonous.[3]

County Superintendent

The office of County Superintendent, which had been abolished during the Finger Administration, was restored in 1897. Said Mebane:

---

[2] Biennial Report, 1896-98, p. 9.

[3] *Ibid.*, pp. 53, 54.

72

The County Superintendent owes his election to county officers. Let's break away from the 'Court House ring' and let the Superintendent render his account to the teachers, children, and parents in the interest and progess of public education regardless of party.[4]

On Taxation

Mebane thought that the General Assembly had done about all it could do to increase the public school fund according to Constitutional limitation. Chapter 421, Laws of 1897, provided special taxation by which amounts raised voluntarily by counties would be duplicated by the State Treasury. Under this provision $8,596.63 had been raised and duplicated by the State.

In a letter sent out to all counties February 28, 1898, Superintendent Mebane wrote:

A township becomes a special school district when a donation is put into the hands of the County Treasurer for the benefit of all the public schools, white and colored; and this is supplemented by the State. By local taxes, the strong help the weak. Local tax is one way by which the BROTHERHOOD OF MAN is forceably brought before the public.[5]

Scope of Mebane's Reports

Charles William Dabney, in his book "Universal Education," rightly says that Mebane's reports were the best since those of Superintendent Calvin H. Wiley.[6] He did indeed cover many phases of education in his reports which indicate the dynamic leadership of the man in his zeal to motivate the public interest toward the schools. His reports include a comprehensive sketch of the schools and the activities of his predecessors since Reconstruction. They note the progress of higher institutions and exhibit pictures of them, including those of the Negro private institutions. Addresses of prominent educators to professional organizations are also included. In addition to and aside from his rather extensive report of statistics, his philosophy, expressed in his introductory remarks before each year's report, would seem to indicate that Mebane was a liberal and an educational statesman.

Changes In School Law

Three important changes in the School Law were enacted during the Biennium, 1896-98: First, The Township Unit was placed under

---

[4] Biennial Report, 1898-1900, pp. 4, 6.

[5] Biennial Report, 1896-98, pp. 43, 44.

[6] Dabney, Op. Cit., p. 214.

73

the management of five school committeemen. A consolidation plan would abolish some small for larger school houses, thus uniting small schools into one strong school with energetic live teachers. Secondly, elections were to be held in every township in the State and any township voting to tax itself $500 would receive the same from the State. Thirdly, a higher estimate of teachers' salaries would be set up under the State Superintendent. Mebane said:

> Local taxation is the only hope of Education to move from 12 weeks to 26 weeks. It would make North Carolina one of the most intelligent instead of one of the most illiterate states.[7]

The Colored Normals

Not discounting the great work done by private institutions like Shaw, Biddle, Saint Augustine's and Livingstone (and some smaller schools), the reader must understand that the colored normals, so far as public education among Negroes was concerned, were the bulwark of the public schools. At least they were the creation of the State, although the State had not yet owned the buildings where these normals existed.

Even though they were charged with the task of training teachers for the public schools, a great part of their work should have been done in the graded schools.

Mebane was not satisfied altogether with the results of these normals. He thought a great deal of the work was not thorough and that there was too much haste to move from fundamentals in order to teach Latin, Algebra, and other higher branches for which, quote: "Most colored teachers will never have any use"; yet Mebane is quoted further as saying:

> I would not have any objection to higher branches if the lower studies were mastered first. Let the money we spend for seven normals be used for three and have the best brains and talent to be found among colored teachers. I would rather be able to send out one good strong well trained teacher to a whole county than to send out to the same county twenty-four poorly trained, weak teachers who know not and know not that they know not. In a few years we will have a class of teachers of power and ability.

Mebane recommended that the seven normals be reduced to three; to be located at Fayetteville, Elizabeth City, and at Winston. His recommendation was concurred with by J. L. M. Curry, Agent for the Peabody Fund, which was a generous contributor to the colored normals. Said Dr. Curry:

---

[7] Biennial Report, 1896-98, p. 75.

We need to get rid of incompetence among both white and colored schools; to divorce from politics and mere selfishness, and give children the benefit of men and women who know how and what to teach.[8]

These schools could not be abolished on the spur of the moment. In fact it was several years after Mebane's recommendation and after his retirement that they were reduced to three. The fact that the State did not yet own the property where these schools existed and that there had been several shiftings from one city to another, plus a lot of bickering among Negro educators for location of normals in their cities made some of these normals rather unstable and the reduction inevitable.*

The Normals listed for the term, 1896-97 and their principals were as follows: Salisbury Normal, John O. Crosby, Principal; Slater Normal at Winston, S. G. Atkins, Principal; Elizabeth City Normal, P. W. Moore, Principal; Franklinton Normal, John A. Savage, Principal; Fayetteville Normal, L. E. Fairley, Principal; Plymouth Normal, J. W. McDonald, Principal; and Goldsboro Normal, P. W. Russell, Principal.[9]

The report as of January 1898 of the State Normal School at Goldsboro was signed by E. E. Smith, Principal*

In chronicling excerpts of the reports of these normal schools, some of the names of individuals are mentioned partly because they have come down to the current era as educators or because some of them were known to the writer or because of special mention by their principal.

Franklinton Normal, 1896-97

There were 258 students coming from 27 counties in this year and 10 teachers employed. Industrial training was part of the curriculum and a requirement of the Senior Class was a First Grade Certificate. The chief objective of the normal was to improve rural teaching. The school owned $10,000 worth of property free from any encumbrance. For the term, 1897-98 the enrollment was 268; in 1898-99, 279; and in 1900 had reached 300. The report mentions the visitation of a Mrs. F. D. Palmer, who had given the farm; a Dr.

* We do know that E. E. Smith had two leaves of absence from Fayetteville State Normal; one during his appointment as U. S. Minister to Liberia; the other during his service in the Spanish American War.

[8] *Ibid.,* p. 15.

* The New Bern Normal had been moved to Goldsboro; Franklinton Normal had been moved to Warrenton and later moved back to Franklinton; several towns in the East tried to secure the Plymouth Normal, among them being Winton, where C. S. Brown was principal of Waters Institute.

[9] *Ibid.,* p. 138.

Blood of Pennsylvania; Professor Williams, of the Blind School; and S. H. Vick of Wilson.[10]*

Salisbury Normal 1896-97

The enrollment for the term, 1896-97 was 134 students representing 15 counties. In 1898 the enrollment was 162. For many years the Salisbury Normal was said to be first in thoroughness. During the summer of 1900, a school was conducted for 112 teachers who came from several counties of the State and some from the State of Virginia. The assistants at this summer session were L. E. Fairly and P. W. Moore. The Superintendent of the schools in Salisbury at the time was C. L. Coon, who is remembered in later years as Superintendent in Wilson. The principal was John O. Crosby.[11]

Although the Salisbury Normal was said to have been first in thoroughness, Mebane thought there was no need of a normal at Salisbury as Livingstone College was there. He had previously recommended the number of normals decreased and the efficiency increased.[12]

Goldsboro Normal, 1896-97

The only important note in the report for 1896-97 was a request for an additional teacher. It was signed by E. E. Smith, Principal. During the 18th Annual session which closed May 11, 1900, there was an enrollment of 101 students and 3 graduates. H. E. Hagans was the principal.[13]

Plymouth Normal 1896-98

The session of 1896-97, the 16th annual, enrolled 175 students. The principal, H. C. Crosby, died between the 16th and the 17th Annual Sessions. J. W. McDonald became the principal. The assistant teachers were listed as Mrs. E. J. Dance, R. R. Cartwright, E. H. Corprew and the Reverend J. E. Cordon. The term of 1897-98 had an enrollment of 205.[14]

---

[10] Biennial Report, 1896-98 and 1898-1900, pp. 165, 192. Foot note: Hartshorn, Era of Progress and Promise, p. 208.

* (ff. While the State supported this normal school, the institution actually was a Presbyterian school, founded as Albion Academy in 1887. Its first principal was Moses Hopkins).

[11] Biennial Report, 1898-1900, p. 195.

[12] Ibid., pp. 4, 6.

[13] Ibid., p. 188.

[14] Ibid., p. 159.

Slater Normal, Winston, 1896-97

The report, dated June 7, 1897, stated that the school had been organized only two years and had no graduates that year. There were 78 students enrolled in the Normal Department. In cooperation with the Slater Industrial, one of the strongest teachers of the State had been added. The enrollment in 1898 was 95 males and 150 females. The school was reported as having high moral tones. The teachers were active Christian workers. The names of H. E. Fries and W. A. Blair, long to be remembered by citizens of Winston-Salem, were mentioned as great friends of the school. S. G. Atkins, Principal.

Dr. Atkins reported institutes held at Winston, Plymouth, and at Goldsboro during the summer of 1898. At Winston, 70 teachers enrolled; at Goldsboro 181; and At Plymouth, 138. He stated:

The teachers seemed to have their faces toward the rising sun.

The report lists, among those associated in the institutes, the names of J. H. Michael, The Reverend O. Faduma, a native born African, C. G. O'Kelley, W. F. Fonveille, C. Dillard, P. W. Moore, and W. T. Whitted.[15]

New Bern, 1898-1900

Although New Bern no longer had a State Normal school, a report dated September 10, 1900 showed an enrollment of 101 students and mentions the names of instructors as W. A. Byrd, W. G. Avant, and C. Dillard.[16]

Elizabeth City Normal, 1896-98

P. W. Moore, Principal, reported 162 enrolled in 1896-97 and 11 graduates. Fifty-three of these enrollees were already teachers. He listed the following as student teachers who taught one or more classes a day: Miss H. S. Rayner, Mrs. Georgianna Harrell, Miss M. E. Mebane, Miss M. E. Brockett, Miss M. E. Leuter, Isaiah Williams, W. H. Parker, G. R. Whitfield, and J. F. Pierce.[17]

In his report of June 8, 1900, Moore listed his assistants as Miss Anna M. Brochies and Joshua R. Fleming. He mentioned Thomas S. Cooper of Bertie as a prize winner for the best oration at Commencement. Others mentioned as prize winners were: Miss A. L. Brinn, the R. J. Mitchell prize for the best essay; J. Frank Pierce of Bertie for his oration; J. Braxton Lewis, the Ehringhause Brothers and Company prize; Miss Louise M. Brown, the McCabe prize for the

---

[15] *Ibid.*, p. 139 ff.

[16] *Ibid.*, p. 199.

[17] Biennial Report 1896-98, p. 153.

best recital; and Miss Amanda M. Hill, of Tyrell County for the best oration for a second year pupil.[18]

These reports of the normals are recorded through 1900, the final year of the Mebane Administration. They contain names of many leading Negro educators who should be honored and revered by generations to come for the work done in laying so solid a foundation upon which future educators would build.

The names of S. G. Atkins, E. E. Smith, and P. W. Moore are more easily remembered because the institutions with which they were so intimately identified still live as great bulwarks of educational endeavor. Some others, not so easily remembered are listed in reports of these normal schools. In 1900 Principal J. W. McDonald of Plymouth Normal gives special mention to Mrs. S. E. Epps, Mrs. E. J. Dance, Mrs. W. T. Dancy, Mrs. L. W. Perry, and C. M. Epps.[19]

Statistics of the Mebane Administration

School census, enrollment, and attendance figures for 1897 showed the number of white children (6 to 21) as 412,143; colored 211,519. Enrollment, white, 222,252; colored 131,404. Average attendance, white, 110,677; colored, 58,548. The value of white school property was $644,309.75; colored, $234,324. The average monthly salary of white males was $23.21; females $20.81; colored males, $21.54; colored females, $18.25.[20]

Figures for 1898: Census of white children (6 to 21) 415,262; colored, 213,218. Enrolled, white, 216,223; colored 138,152; average attendance, white, 144,346; colored 68,894. The average monthly salaries for white males was $24.66; females $22.96; colored males $21.64; females $19.85.[21]

Despite the heroic efforts of this dedicated State Superintendent, the sad fact remained that half the State's children were still not attending school and the constitutional length of the term in rural sections stood at 4 months.

In assessing the status of Superintendent Mebane's Administration, it is evident that he was deeply conscious of the enormity of the educational problems of the times and that he was profoundly dedicated to the almost hopeless task of solving them. In recognizing the role and influence of the ministers of the Gospel, he said:

> It is a fact that ministers of the Gospel can and do reach and influence some parents with reference to their duty to their children more than any other persons can. Many have

---

[18] Biennial Report 1898-1900, p. 170.

[19] *Ibid.*, p. 184.

[20] Biennial Report 1896-1900, p. 278.

[21] *Ibid.*, p. 289.

preached the gospel of education in the pulpit and in the home and have done much for the cause of education.[22]

As he approached the end of this term, he wrote the following, which this writer would term a "solemn valedictory":

> For four year, I have tried to do my duty to the children of this State, but how little, it seems to me, I have accomplished; but I shall not worry about results, if the future historians can truly write of me, "He was faithful to the trust imposed upon him and did what he could for the welfare of the children." Then, I am content.[23]

---

[22] Biennial Report 1898-1900, p. 59.

[23] *Ibid.*, p. 72.

Chapter VII

The Toon - Joyner Administration

1900 - 1918

Thomas F. Toon was elected to the State Superintendency in September 1900. He assumed office January 1, 1901, but died thirteen months thereafter, February 12, 1902. James Yadkin Joyner was appointed by Governor Aycock to succeed him as State Superintendent.

Since Toon could not have submitted a biennial report, the short time of his service is covered under the biennial reports submitted by his successor. The Joyner Administration therefore, covers a longer period than that of any of his predecessors. It embraces an era of North Carolina history remarkable in its extent and in the events which characterized the period. It covers the period when the Nation was just emerging from the Spanish-American War, the intensity of the Campaign for Universal Education, the disfranchisement of Negroes, and World War I.

The impact of the period upon the Equality of Education among Negroes may have been influenced by the disfranchisement. However controversial the elimination of Negroes from politics may have been, it is certain that Universal Education was a soothing challenge to the Negro's ambition. Under Charles E. Aycock as Governor, or James Y. Joyner, as State Superintendent, Negroes had a "friend at court."

Born in LaGrange, Lenoir County, Joyner had been associated with many of the leading men in North Carolina education. He was associated with former State Superintendent Wiley in the organization of the graded school at Winston; had been Superintendent of schools in Lenoir County; had succeeded Alderman as Superintendent of Schools in Goldsboro; had headed the English Department at the N. C. College for Women in Greensboro; and had conducted institutes in a number of counties.[1]

In the introduction of his first Biennial Report, Joyner paid tribute to his predecessor, General Thomas F. Toon:

As a leader of the forces of light and knowledge in the battle against the forces of darkness and ignorance, he manifested the same patriotic zeal, the same dauntless courage, and the same devotion to duty that had won for him the

---

[1] N. C. Biographers, by Special Staff of Writers, ''Rebuilding An Ancient Commonwealth,'' p. 407.

love and everlasting gratitude of his people long years before on the field of blood and carnage.

In calling the public attention to the powers of education to create wealth and to develop the resources of intellectual and moral power, Joyner boldly warned against denying these truths in their application to Negroes on the premise that the white race pays the greater part of taxation:

> Why should not the taxes of the rich, because they pay more taxes than the poor, be used for the education of the rich; and taxes of the poor for the education of the poor?[2]

On The Education of the Negro

Joyner thought that North Carolina had made mistakes in its method and activities of educating the Negro and that it was incumbent upon the State to demonstrate by a better and more effective sort of education that may be more helpful to him and to the whites before it is possible to convince many white people that education, even of the right sort, is good for the (n)egro. (sic) He thought that the best training for Negroes was in agriculture, but that mastery of the essentials of knowledge was necessary for every individual.

Joyner came into office in the thick of the campaign to disfranchise the Negro. Commenting thereon, in the face of threats to deny education as well as the franchise, Joyner sounded off:

> That to take away the Negro's right of suffrage and then deprive him by constitutional amendment of the means of ever acquiring fitness for exercising suffrage would do violence to the consciences of the civilized world and would be an act of injustice unworthy of a great and generous race.
>
> There seems no end to this great and vexing problem, but I have abiding faith that this great, just, and generous Anglo-Saxon race in North Carolina will take courage to work out this problem in a spirit of equity to both races and will in the future as in the past, command the admiration of the world by its magnanimous treatment of a weaker race.[3]

The other "Friend at Court" for the Negro was none other than Governor Aycock. Having removed the Negro from politics, extremists sought by legislative action to curtail his education by a proposed amendment to the Constitution which would divide the funds derived from school taxes between the races on the basis of what each race paid. Aycock declared that he would resign the gover-

---

[2] Biennial Reports, 1900-1904, p. 72.

[3] Ibid., p. 34 ff.

norship if such an amendment were passed. He attacked the proposal as viciously as he had advocated Universal Education. The proposal was killed when it came to a vote.[4]

Argument concerning tax division by race persisted with nearly every election campaign, although the proposed amendment had failed in 1905. Nevertheless, in 1910, five years after the failure of passage, Joyner felt it necessary to renew his efforts in mollifying the tempers of the extremists for the proposal:

> In justice to the Negro and for the information of some (whites) who have been misled into thinking that too large a part of the taxes white people pay is spent for the education of the Negro; under Section 4116 of the School Law, apportionment of the school fund in each county is practically placed under the control of the County Board of Education; the only restriction laid upon the Board being that the funds shall be apportioned among schools of each township in such a way as to give equal length of term as nearly as possible, having due regard to grade of work to be done, the qualification of teachers, etc.
>
> The Constitution directs that in the distribution of funds no discrimination shall be made in favor of either race . . . the Negroes constitute 32 per cent of the school population and receive 16 per cent of the school money . . . they pay in taxes on their own property and polls (not including corporations) about $190,378.81 or less than one half of what they receive for school purposes. Add to this their share of fines, forfeitures and penalties plus their share of the large school tax paid by corporations, the amount paid by whites for Negro education is so small that the man who would begrudge or complain about it ought to be ashamed of himself.[5]

Educational Revival, 1902-04

The most outstanding development of the early Joyner period was the CAMPAIGN FOR EDUCATION which coincided with the Aycock program of Universal Education. The campaign in North Carolina grew out of a series of national conferences on Education held around the turn of the Century; three of which had been held at Capon Springs, West Virginia. These conferences included some of the leading philanthropists of the nation. A fourth conference was held at Winston-Salem in April 1901. It included John D. Rockefeller, Jr., Robert C. Odden, and Governor Aycock. Out of its deliberations was formed the Southern Education Board which in turn gave rise

---

[4] Dabney, *Op. Cit.* p. 217 ff.

[5] Biennial Report, 1910-12, p. 54.

to the General Education Board.[6] Before the story ends, much will be said as to the impact of these great educational boards upon Negro Education.

The Campaign for Education in North Carolina was to be waged vigorously in every county. It received impetus from many notables in the field of education. Walter Hines Page, said that there was enough native intelligence going to waste in North Carolina for lack of training to govern the entire world.

The Southern Education Board and the General Education Board cooperated in defraying the expense of a summer campaign in 1902 and also travel expenses of county superintendents to a conference at Raleigh November 12-14, 1902. Superintendents from 84 counties attended. They had met for serious business and out of the meeting was organized the State Association of County Superintendents. The Conference also provided for five district associations. Joyner urged the county Boards to send their superintendents annually and to provide for their expenses to the meetings.

An educational platform was adopted February 13, 1903. It was reaffirmed in Greensboro on April 3 and later at Charlotte on May 2 and at Morehead City by The Teachers Assembly June 13. Following are excerpts of that platform:[7]

> Be it resolved that an active and vigorous campaign be inaugurated in every county for the accomplishment of the following ends:
>
> 1. Consolidation of small districts wherever possible
> 2. Erection of adequate and comfortable school houses
> 3. Lengthening of public school term by taxation

Recommendations, 1908-10

Several progressive recommendations were noted in Joyner's report of 1908-1910 which included: Organizing Farm Life Schools to seek to improve appreciation and practicality of rural living; requiring summer schools of higher institutions without tuition charge; raising the salaries of Second Grade teachers from $25 to $30 per month; requiring attendance of teachers at county institutes; amending the law to enable special-tax districts to increase the length of terms; and organizing and developing high schools. Private high schools, he said, could not meet the standard of competition with public high schools. He further recommended industrial and agricultural training as a necessary function to meet the multitudinous tasks of the practical work of the world for all the normal schools and the A. and M. College.[8]

---

[6] Brown, *Op. Cit.*, p. 41.

[7] Biennial Report 1902-04, Part III, p. 215.

[8] Biennial Report 1908-10, p. 28.

The Campaign For Education continued under the leadership of Joyner who was ably assisted by Governor Glenn, ex-Governor Aycock, former Superintendent Mebane, Henry E. Fries and others. Educational bulletins, press releases, and public addresses kept the campaign constantly before the public. In 1906 Joyner announced a Conference For Education in the South to be held March 26, 1907 at Pinehurst.[9]

Legislation

Several legislative acts of the long Joyner Administration deserve more than passing notice. First, an Act to encourage the establishment of libraries in the public schools of the rural districts:

> Any district raising $10 by private subscription will be matched by the County Board of Education out of money belonging to the District; said money to be refunded by the State Board.

This Act was ratified March 13, 1901. A committee to select suitable books consisted of the following: E. P. Moses, D. H. Hill, J. J. Foust, B. F. Sledd, G. A. Grimsley, and T. F. Toon.

Secondly, an Act to appropriate Two Hundred Thousand Dollars to Public Schools was enacted and ratified March 11, 1901:

1. $100,000 to be appropriated annually out of the State Treasury for the benefit of public schools to be distributed to the counties per capita as to school census.

2. Superintendents to issue warrants upon the State Auditor for amounts due in favor of the County Treasury to the credit of the School Fund.

3. That the sum of $100,000 be applied for the purpose of bringing the school term up to the Constitutional requirement of 4 months.

The money was to be applied without discrimination to Negro and Indian schools as well as to white schools.[11]

First Mention of Newbold

As far as Negro educators were concerned, the most honored and revered personality to rise to prominence during the Joyner regime was N. C. Newbold. The first mention we note of Newbold is in a report of Superintendent F. H. Curtis. Newbold assisted him in

---

[9] Biennial Report 1906-08, p. 187.

[10] Biennial Report 1900-04, p. 198

[11] *Ibid.*, p. 131 ff.

conducting an "Excellent Normal School" for a month at Asheboro for the rural schools of the county.[12]

The magnificent contribution of N. C. Newbold to the education of Negroes in North Carolina will be given appropriate coverage later on in the story.*

Other Legislation

Various steps which mark the progress of the long Joyner tenure are discussed in Section 4116 of SCHOOL LAWS OF 1905 (Repealed 1919). These laws provided that counties shall set aside 1/6, if necessary, of the total school funds to be used in securing a 4-months term in every school in the county and that

The Governor, Lieutenant Governor, State Treasurer, State Auditor, State Superintendent of Public Instruction, and the Attorney-General shall constitute the State Board of Education and are created a corporation.[13]

Maximum Teachers' Pay, White and Colored

The following schedule was the maximum amount allowed by law for the salaries of teachers for 4 months in white and colored schools in respective schools asking for aid from the second One Hundred Thousand Dollars, adopted in 1901 to guarantee the 4-months School Term:[14]

1. Actual enrollment of 70 or less, white schools, not more than $113.44
   Actual enrollment of 70 or less, colored schools, not more than $90.52

2. Actual enrollment 70 to 105 employing 2 teachers (white) $226.88
   Actual enrollment 70 to 105 employing 2 teachers (colored) $181.04

3. Actual enrollment 105 to 140 employing 3 teachers (white) $340.32
   Actual enrollment 105 to 140 employing 3 teachers (colored) $244.00

High Schools

The General Assembly in 1907 appropriated $45,000 from the State Treasury to aid in establishing public high schools for the rural

---

[12] Ibid., p. 379.

* See Brown, A History of the Education of Negroes in North Carolina, Chapter V, "Era of Newbold."

[13] Pell's Revisal 1908, Volume II, p. 2040.

[14] Biennial Report 1902-04, p. 222

districts. Although no mention is made of race in the report concerning this Act, Negro children did not benefit from the high school appropriation. The report states that during the first year following the Act, 156 high schools were established in 81 counties. They were supervised by a high school inspector who devoted his entire time to this function. During the first year 3,949 rural boys and girls were enrolled.[15]

In 1909-10 there were 175 public high schools in the rural districts with an enrollment of 7,000 pupils and buildings with a total value of $123,000 had been erected. There were only 9 counties without public high schools; viz., Brunswick, Chowan, Dare, New Hanover, Pasquotank, Perquimans, Stanley, Tyrell, and Yancey. The public high school for Wayne County was moved from Goldsboro to Pikeville.[16]

Aside from high school work done in private academies and in some larger city schools, the only secondary school courses available to Negro students were in the preparatory departments of the colleges. Indeed, for a good many years, high school subjects for Negroes were almost officially prohibitive.

N. W. Walker, Professor of Secondary Education at the University of North Carolina, in his report, PUBLIC HIGH SCHOOLS, wrote as follows:

> The public high schools are now pretty well dispersed over the State — literally from Currituck to Cherokee.

His third report, dated November 21, 1910, showed increases in enrollment, in number of teachers, in salaries, and in general improvement. The report does not mention any Negro high schools. In his recommendations, 1909, 1910, he urged the adoption of the following proposals:

1. That the County be made the unit of organization and support

2. That the elementary school be segregated from the central high school and thus free it from dominance by high school influence

3. That two years of high school be continued

4. That the State appropriation be increased

By 1910 Wayne County had 3 public high schools: Falling Creek, J. F. Thompson, Principal; Pikeville, A. R. Freeman, Principal; and Seven Springs, W. J. Sloan, Principal. Wake County had 4 public high schools: Cary, M. E. Dry, Principal; Bay Leaf at Route 1, Neuse, F. L. Foust, Principal; Holy Springs, K. H. McIntyre, Principal; and Wakelon at Zebulon, R. C. Holton, Principal.

---

[15] Biennial Report 1906-08, p. 9.

[16] Walker, N. W., *Public High Schools*, Part III, p. 9.

There were towns and village public high schools in most communities of the State. W. C. Jackson headed the Greensboro Public High School; H. P. Harding, Charlotte; E. J. Green, Durham; J. L. Hathcock, Goldsboro; Z. D. McWhorten, Mount Olive, W. H. Coltrane, North Wilkesboro; and Hugh Morson, Raleigh.[17]*

Joyner and Industrial Training

Joyner believed that the foundation of all education was the mastery of the rudiments of knowledge: reading, writing, and arithmetic; and that it must be well laid. His philosophy on the subject follows:

> Every wise system of education . . . must recognize natural differences of endowment and tastes, thus cooperating with nature and God. The education that turns a life into unnatural channels dooms it to inevitable failure and tragedy.
>
> In recognition of these established laws of nature and life, manual training and industrial education are beginning to find a fixed and permanent place in systems of modern education. They have already been given a place in some of the higher institutions of our public school system in the A. and M. College at Raleigh, State Normal and Industrial for Women at Greensboro and at the A. and M. College for colored at Greensboro.[18]

The writer pauses here to remind the reader of the mention of Mebane's philosophy of Industrial Education compared with that of Booker T. Washington in Chapter VI. These men were more prophetic in their views than many Negro educators are able to appreciate even in this age of automation — a premise to anticipate in later chapters on Quality Education.

Graded Schools

In the cities and towns where graded schools had been established, Negro children received generally the same benefits as white children. However, the length of term in some localities was slightly shorter and the facilities were generally much inferior. In addition teachers' salaries were lower for Negro teachers.

As noted in an earlier chapter, Greensboro had set the stage for Graded Schools as early as 1870 and its charter permitted no distinction between the races as to division of school funds. With a population of 10,055 in 1900, Greensboro had 1,302 white and 1,666 colored

---

[17] *Ibid.*, p. 54 ff.

* Some of these names are well remembered by present day educators and some have schools named for them.

[18] Biennial Report 1904-06, p. 52 ff.

children in its graded schools. The Superintendent at the time, Edgar D. Broadhurst, gave 5 hours per week to teaching. His salary was $1,500. The value of school property was $4 million. The average monthly salary of white male teachers was $67.50; Negro male, $45; white women teachers, $37.50; Negro women, $25. There were 10 grades for the white children; 7 for Negro children.

During the Joyner Administration, graded schools had become well established. Asheville in 1900 had a city population of 14,694. Its graded school enrolled 2,604 white and 1,298 Negro children. There were 10 grades for white and 8 for Negro children. The average salary for white men teachers was $675 annually; for colored men teachers, $550 annually; White women, $420; Colored women $316.

Charlotte had a city population of 19,902. There were 3,401 white and 2,224 colored children enrolled in its graded schools. The length of term was given as 36 weeks; number of grades, 10; and the finances were not separated by race.

In Durham the average annual salary for white men was reported as $750; Negro men as $500; white women as $385; and colored women as $260.

The Goldsboro Graded Schools in 1900 had 4 buildings valued at $50,000; furniture, $6,000; apparatus, $1,000; Library with 3,000 volumes, valued at $1,500. The number of grades was 10. The Superintendent gave his entire time to office and supervision. His salary was $1,500 annually. E. B. Borden was Chairman of the Board.

Fayetteville reported its population as 7,000 with 1,000 white and 1,066 colored children enrolled in its graded schools. The Superintendent, J. A. Jones, gave 5 hours per week to teaching and 25 hours to supervision. His salary was $800.

Several other cities were listed in the reports contained in the Biennial Report of 1900-1904, but those mentioned here are examples of the movement which by 1900 had become firmly established.[19]

Colored Normal Schools

As was indicated in Chapter VI, the number of normal schools had been reduced to three. This reduction of the normals should not be construed to indicate any curtailment of the State's obligation to Negro education, but should be regarded as an honest effort to insure the Quality of the program. Obviously, the State was in no position to spread its appropriation adequately over seven such schools and get the best results. It had already abolished the white normals; so to keep three of the colored and abolish four should have seemed no injustice to Negro education.

Joyner included in his recommendations, the consolidation of the seven normals into three to be located at Fayetteville, Elizabeth City, and Winston-Salem and to establish manual training and agricultural

---

[19] Biennial Report 1900-04, p. 210 ff.

activities as part of their curriculum.[20] He also included later on in his recommendations that an amount of $5,000 annually be appropriated for buildings and equipment and to develop departments of Domestic Science and Industrial Training. He noted that there were neither houses nor permanent plants belonging to the State and that the amount of $3,250 annual appropriation was hardly enough to pay annual expenses.[21]

Final reports of the normals which were abolished are noted in the Biennials of 1900 and 1904. Goldsboro Normal made its annual report June 30, 1902, showing its financial account signed by W. T. Hollowell, Secretary-Treasurer. The school had enrolled 133 students in 1901-02. Two thirds of them held teachers' certificates from 14 different counties. There was no senior class during that term and hence no graduates. The aim of the school, the report stated, was to strive to give thorough training in the essentials. Industrial work for boys and girls had been instituted. The Principal was H. E. Hagans.[22]

Franklinton Normal

The school enrolled 301 pupils in 1901-02. They represented 51 counties. Industrial training had been instituted. There were 16 graduates listed as follows:

Hattie V. Murphy of Elm City, Lucy Person of Letha, N. C., Bessie Sessoms of Rocky Mount, Melvin Arrington of Hillardstown, N. C., Richard Blue of Red Springs, James L. Brown of Laurinburg, James H. Bynum of Wilson, Julius C. Chance of Williamston, John A. Evans of Louisburg, Guilford F. Fuller of Mountain Hills, N. C., A. T Hawkins of Letha, N. C., R. O. Hooper of Lumberton, James F. McKay of Dunn, Julius R. McKnight of Franklinton, Alonzo R. Phillips of Wilson, W. A. Watson of Whitakers, Theo Mays of Lillington and Fairley C. Malloy.

The report showed the total finances from all sources as $6,000. There were no debts but the salaries were too small. J. A. Savage, Principal.[23]

Franklinton Normal was abolished June 1905, but the school continued under its original set up as Albion Academy until 1933 when it was merged with two other Presbyterian schools.[24]

---

[20]*Ibid.*, p. LXII, Intro. Remarks

[21] *Ibid.*, p. 22.

[22] *Ibid.*, pp. 75, 355.

[23] *Ibid.*, p. 351.

[24] Brown, *Op. Cit.*, p. 37.

Plymouth Normal

There were 192 students enrolled during the term, 1901-02. A dormitory for girls had been erected and there were three students graduated in 1901. They were Mary W. Webb of Plymouth, Arthur E. Hudson* of Tarboro, and W. W. Walker of Plymouth.

The following are listed as graduates in 1902: McKoy Lawrence of Leggettes, Frank Jones of Plymouth, Milton L. Armstead of Plymouth, Eugene G. Armstead of Plymouth, and Mamie S. Hill of Sunbury. The report was signed, C. M. Eppes,[25] Superintendent. Eppes made a strong plea for the retention of the normal at Plymouth which had been in existence for twenty years.[26]

Professor Eppes, as he was familiarly known, was a conspicuous personality in educational, civic, and fraternal circles for many years. He served as principal for the colored schools of Greenville and the present high school is named in his honor.

Salisbury Normal

The final report from the Salisbury Normal was made on June 12, 1903. During that year the school enrolled 198 students who represented 33 counties. There were 29 graduates. The Normal was abolished in 1903 and its equipment that had any value was sold to Livingstone College and to Dr. J. O. Crosby, principal of the Normal.

Fayetteville Normal

The first of the colored normals was one of the three retained in compliance with the recommendation of both Mebane and Joyner. In 1901-02, the school enrolled 135 students of whom 59 held teachers' certificates and had already taught in public schools. There were no graduates that year because another year had been added to the curriculum. The report lists as instructors: Edward Evans, J. F. K. Simpson, Rowena Jacobs, and Mamie Waddell.[27]

By 1910 a new brick dormitory for girls was opened and the school enrolled 338 students. The instruction was considerably improved as many of the Faculty were attending summer schools in New York, at Hampton Institute, and other recognized summer schools. The assistant teachers were products of such institutions as Shaw University, Lincoln University, and Fisk University. A practice

---

* Arthur E. Hudson is currently a Presiding Elder in the AME Zion Church, residence, Goldsboro.

[25] Biennial Report 1902-04, p. 353.

[26] Ibid., p. 543.

[27] Ibid., p. 357.

school had been built and domestic science and art had been instituted. E. E. Smith was the principal.[28]

At the close of the Joyner regime, 1918, Fayetteville State Normal had become well entrenched in the educational program for Negroes in the State. Aside from a regular enrollment of 285 students, there were 231 teachers enrolled in its summer school in 1918. The school had a well equipped industrial facility for both men and women students.[29]

Elizabeth City State Normal

In the early 1900's, this institution was rapidly becoming well established under the sterling leadership of P. W. Moore. In 1901 there were 150 teachers enrolled in its summer school and 49 students in the regular session. In 1902-03 the regular session enrolled 69 and the summer school, 150. Moore believed in giving his reports a little personal touch by listing names of students who had done something outstanding. Some of those who were awarded prizes at commencement are listed as follows: 1st prize, Miss A. O. Wilson of Currituck; 2nd, Miss M. L. Sessoms of Bertie; and 3rd, Miss Emma L. McDougald of Columbus. Names of graduates are listed as follows: Louise Brown of Trenton, Amanda Hill of Columbia, Clotee Brinkley of Norfolk, Virginia, Bertha Hawkins of Corapeake, Annie Jones of Elizabeth City, Thomas J. Raynor of Windsor, Lucius Starke of Elizabeth City, Thomas S. Cooper of Windsor, Emma L. McDougald of Whiteville, Mamie L. Sessoms of Windsor, John Brockett of Elizabeth City, Henry Outlaw of Bertie, John P. Law of Bertie, and Corlee Little of Edenton.[30]

One of the Normal's best instructors who later became its Principal was J. C. Bias, Professor of Mathematics. He resigned in 1910 to accept a position at Shaw University. Bias returned to the institution as Dean in 1921 and upon the retirement of Moore in 1928 became the Principal.

In 1908-09 the school enrolled 347 students who came from 25 different counties of the State. There were 24 normal graduates in that year.[31] By 1918, the enrollment reached 473 of which 236 were summer school teachers. An industrial building had been erected through the generosity of the General Education Board.[32]

---

[28] Biennial Report 1910-12, p. 98.

[29] Biennial Report 1916-18, Part III, p. 107.

[30] Biennial Report 1900-04, p. 345.

[31] Biennial Report 1908-10, p. 134.

[32] Biennial Report 1916-18, Part III, p. 104.

In 1900 Slater Normal reached an enrollment of only 86 regular students, 152 practice school children, and 18 special students for a total of 256. All normal students were receiving some industrial training. About 100 teachers were attending its summer school. Some of the graduates of 1901 are listed as follows: Lemuel Banks, Mittie Brown, L. V. Brown, all of Winston-Salem; Walter C. Bryan of Tarboro; Mary L. Mosely of Madison; Callie Hairston, Charles J. Hairston, and John T. Martin of Winston; Grace J. Peters of Raleigh, John A. Rousseau of Wilkesboro and John M. Smith of Wilson.[33]

In 1908 there were 88 students, ten teachers and officers. These students came from 24 different counties and from several other states. C. G. O'Kelley was the Principal in the absence of S. G. Atkins.

In 1910, F. M. Kennedy was acting as Principal. During his time electric current and steam heating were installed and four lots near the school were purchased. Kennedy advocated the teaching of agriculture and carpentry and sponsoring an annual colored fair.[34]

Atkins returned to the institution in 1913 and found it with a healthy growth. A building which had been used as a hospital for the Slater Industrial School had been acquired and a girls' dormitory had been approved. Two hundred thousand bricks had been made in anticipation of the new dormitory.

Atkins reported that Slater Normal graduates were found teaching in some of the leading schools of the State and that the leading Negro contractor in Winston was a graduate of Slater. He stated further, "Our teachers are concerned about the quality of the work done."[35]

By 1918 Slater Normal had enrolled 652 students, including summer school teachers and had erected a $20,000 industrial building for boys. A diversified high school course followed by normal instruction was adopted. The school was active in various types of war-time work among both students and teachers.[36]

A. and M College, Greensboro

In 1902 instruction at the A. and M. College was limited to male students; domestic science and art having been discontinued. The curriculum consisted of mechanical art, agricultural industries, and trade teaching. A farm of 100 acres valued at $50,000 had been acquired and graduates were being profitably employed at earning of from $30 to $50 per month. The attendance in 1902 was 116; the loss

---

[33] Biennial Report 1900-02, p. 360.

[34] Biennial Report 1910-12, p. 93.

[35] Biennial Report 1908-10, Part II, pp. 50, 52.

[36] Biennial Report 1916-18, Part III, p. 101.

of female students having reduced the enrollment to about half of that of the previous year. Principal James B. Dudley recommended a department to train rural teachers with agricultural training.[37]

Deaf and Blind Institution

The head of the colored department was Dr. M. D. Bowen in 1902 and the supervisor was Charles M. Williams; girls' matron was Eliza Dunston; boys', Mary J. Warren. Others listed in the colored department were Lucy M. Davis, Blanche W. Williams, Alice V. Williams, William Quinn, William Wilder, and James Shepherd. Domestic Science and other practical courses were taught and exhibits of the colored department were shown at the Colored State Fair, taking some 25 premiums in competition with those of colored schools and colleges over the State.[38]

N. C. Newbold

The story of the long regime of James Y. Joyner could not be complete without chronicling the magnificent work of N. C. Newbold, an ardent advocate of equality in the education of Negroes. (See Brown, *A History of the Education of Negroes,* Chapter V.)

No man in all North Carolina educational history was more dedicated to his task than Newbold. It was the great privilege of the writer to know Newbold personally. He was a man with a frail body, but with a great mind and an understanding heart. He maintained the confidence of both white and Negro citizens and, although his activities extended long after the passing of Joyner, his work was no less outstanding with Joyner.

Newbold was appointed by Joyner as State Agent for rural schools in 1913. His first objective was to have industrial work taught in the county institutes. Next, to contact the superintendents in the 19 counties where Jeanes Supervisors were employed. This was followed up by consulting Negro leaders as to conditions among the Negro people. The report of his findings was a bold pronouncement. Had the white educators and leaders ever before been addressed in word like these?

The average Negro rural school house is really a disgrace to an independent, civilized people. To one who does not know our history, these school houses, though mute, would tell in unmistaken terms a story of injustice, inhumanity, and neglect on the part of our white people. Such a condition would appear to an observer, uninformed of our past as in-

---

[37] Biennial Report 1900-02, p. 434.

[38] *Ibid.*, p. 479.

N. C. NEWBOLD

First Director of the Division of Negro Education

tolerable, indefensible, unbusiness-like and, above all, un-Christian.[39]

Working with the Jeanes teachers, or as they came to be called, supervisors, and farm leaders, Newbold prepared a course of study for rural schools consisting of practical training in sanitation, health, cooking, sewing, housekeeping, gardening, farming, dairying, poultry management, and manual training all based upon the essential elementary studies. Home-Makers clubs followed the work of the institutes in cooperation with farm and garden demonstration work. Clubs were organized in 14 counties with local county industrial supervisors of Negro schools in charge of the work. Counties paid a part of the salary while the General Education Board supplied the balance.

Newbold's activities were closely identified with the sponsorship of several great philanthorpic funds, viz., the General Education Board, the Jeanes Fund, the Slater Fund, and the Rosenwald School Fund. All of these funds had been profoundly and actively interested generally with education throughout the South while the others were specifically interested in Negro education.

The Slater Fund was instrumental in establishing county training schools as semi-teacher training institutions; the Jeanes Fund, with supervision of rural schools; while the Rosenwald Fund was interested in school houses. Newbold was actually the agent for all of these great philanthropies. There will be more of the activities of Newbold in connection with these funds in the chapter on E. C. Brooks which follows the present chapter.

County Training Schools

The first of the county training schools were the Johnston County Training School at Smithfield, Pamlico County Training School at Stonewall, and the Wake County (Berry O'Kelly) Training School at Method. The establishment of this type of training schools was the basis for the promotion of public high schools for Negroes in the rural districts.[40]

Newbold made a recommendation to the State Board of Education requesting that the State either make a direct appropriation of $5,000 to aid in setting up county training schools or a supplementary amount to be added to the State High School appropriation with the understanding that it would be used for such schools. He said to the Board:

> When we consider the fact that there are no high schools for Negroes in the State and further that there are so few places where the children in these districts can get any

---

[39] Biennial Report 1912-14, Part III, p. 124.

[40] Brown, *Op. Cit.*, p. 55.

training beyond the elementary, it seems to me but just and right that the State should make provisions for schools of this character, at least to the extent that one school of this kind might be established in each county where needed.[41]

The Jeanes Teachers (Supervisors)

The Jeanes teachers were the outgrowth of a liberal minded Quaker lady from Philadelphia who contributed a fund to help Negro rural schools all over the South. Outstanding women teachers, and sometimes men, were selected by the various State Agents to supervise the rural schools in accordance with the Jeanes program.

In 1916 Newbold reported that there were 35 counties in the State with Jeanes teachers. He had visited all the Negro institutions to secure their cooperation in rural work. A Rural School Inspector, C. H. Moore, had been selected and employed by the North Carolina Teachers Association to supervise the work among Negro schools.[42]

The following tabulation shows 3 years of progress among the Jeanes Fund Supervisors:[43]

	1913-14	1914-15	1915-16
Number of Counties with Jeanes Supervisors	19	22	31
Amount paid by Jeanes Fund	$ 4,722.50	$ 4,585.00	$ 6,687.00
Amount paid by counties	1,182.50	1,765.00	3,618.73
Average Length of Term	5.19 mos.	7.08 mos.	5.27 mos.
Number of Schools Extending Term		44	83
Cost of Buildings	17,685.00	14,378.33	25,482.00
Number of School Improvement Leagues	121	207	477
School Grounds Improved	121	310	485
Funds Raised by Negroes	$ 9,393.37	$10,612.32	$15,293.34

Newbold was greatly impressed with the work of Hampton Institute in its program of teacher training. He arranged with the General Education Board to subsidize expenses of County Training School principals for special courses to be taken at Hampton for 4 to 8 weeks. Miss Sarah J. Walter, critic teacher at Hampton, visited the State Normals and some of the county training schools. She was formerly a critic teacher at the Oswego State Normal School, Oswego, New York. Mr. Newbold said of Miss Walter:

She is one of the best qualified critic teachers in the country.[44]*

---

[41] Biennial Report 1914-16, Part III, p. 124.

[42] Ibid., p. 113 ff.

[43] Ibid., p. 111.

[44] Ibid., p. 120.

*The writer was a student under Miss Walter at Hampton.

Summary of the Joyner Era

It is difficult in a single chapter to do justice to the magnitude of the long regime of James Y. Joyner or of the proportions of the Newbold activities under Joyner for there were so many influences, some of which were dedicated men and women, within and without the State. Some of these forces were educational funds consecrated to the great tasks of Universal Education. Other forces are so numerous that time and space prohibit a full appraisal.

One of the great disciples of the era was E. E. Sams, Supervisor of Teacher Training under Joyner. His report on the work of the Normal Schools is an exalted epitome of the philosophy and the spirit of the Joyner regime:

> These schools have been trying to grow and meet the needs and the increasing demands that are being made for better trained and better equipped teachers and leaders among colored people. Believing that the policy . . . for which we have worked is the right one to pursue, namely, the giving of an opportunity to the colored man to develop leadership in harmony with his surroundings and the sympathetic cooperation with his white friends. . . . I urge earnestly that the maintenance fund for the colored normals be made to more nearly meet the needs of these schools. I therefore recommend maintenance for 1915 to be increased from $13,000 to $20,000; and for 1916 and thereafter to $25,000 annually.[45]

One giant stride of the Joyner era was the move from the 4-months to a 6-months term in the rural districts. The Equalizing Fund was created out of revenue derived by setting aside annually 5c of the total annual State Tax levy on each $100 valuation of property for appropriation to the Public Schools of the State; to be used exclusively to pay teachers' salaries, for lengthening the term, and for bringing the school term in every public school district to an equal length; and to a minimum of 6 months, or as near to as the Equalizing Fund will provide.

The previous appropriations of $125,000 and $100,00 were repealed by the Equalization Act and in lieu thereof $250,000 was appropriated to be distributed to the public schools on a per capital basis.[46]

Statistics

School attendance in the final years of the Joyner era indicate clearly that the public schools had benefited greatly from the Campaign For Education. Of the 575,192 white children and 270,872 Ne-

---

[45] Biennial Report 1912-14, Part III, p. 118.

[46] *Ibid.,* p. 20.

gro children (6 to 21) on the school census, 446,370 white and 187,980 Negro children were enrolled in 1918. The per cent of white enrollment was 78 and that of the Negroes, 69.1. However, the per cent of average attendance for white children was 52.3 and that of Negro children, 42.1[47]

The average monthly salaries of teachers also was an indication of the acceptance of the public schools among the citizens of the State. During the Biennium of 1916-18, rural white teachers received an average of $47.27; Negro, $27.53; while in the urban districts, the average white salary was $61.45; Negro $33.81.[48]

James Yadkin Joyner achieved an endearing and lasting place in the hearts of loyal North Carolinians, white and Negro, for his remarkable leadership over a period of sixteen years. Despite pressures from extremists on the race issue, he never retreated from his belief in justice and righteousness. His deeply conceived philosophy that teacher training was the main spring in the development of public schools remained with him to the end. His confidence that the tax question would eventually be resolved without detriment to Negro children was left unshaken. Finally, he lifted the public schools from the brink of hopelessness to a plateau of security upon which a nobler edifice would rise with his successors.

---

[47] Biennial Report 1918-20, p. 80.

[48] Biennial Report 1916-18, p. 42.

Chapter VIII

The Administration of Eugene Clyde Brooks

1919 - 1923

Eugene Clyde Brooks entered upon the State Superintendency at the time when the Nation was emerging from World War I. It was a time when great adjustments both in philosophy and in human relations presented a tremendous challenge to the type of leadership needed in the change-over from a war-time to a peace-time economy.

In cooperation with the war effort, the schools had absorbed many functions which tended to expand the curriculum. Vocational agriculture, and a heightened quality of industrial training (creations of the Smith-Hughes Act of 1917), and health and physical education were partially or indirectly inherited from the war effort.

Aside from these influences, many service men who had been teachers were returning home for jobs they had relinquished to go to war, but fortunately for them the progress of the schools had increased the need for teachers.

Brooks was indeed the man for the times. A forceful speaker and a well informed educator, he was a striking personality before the public. Between 1898 and the decade of the twenties he occupied many positions on the educational ladder He had successfully been a teacher, principal, a city school superintendent, a State Department clerk, a professor of education at Trinity College, State Superintendent of Public Instruction, and President of N. C. State College. He had edited a teacher's magazine and published seven books. He had directed the campaign for better schools under Aycock and was appointed State Superintendent in 1919.[1]

While Brooks' administration was filled with acts of statesmanship generally, it is in that which chiefly demonstrates the remarkable stride toward educational equality of Negro schools that will be the major thesis of this chapter.

The Constitutional Amendment of 1918 which raised the school term to six months was a great boost to rural schools, but the condition of Negro schools was still in a primitive state. Their sad plight was only partially relieved by assistance from the General Education Board, the Rosenwald Fund, and the Jeanes and Slater Boards.[2]

---

[1] William B. Gatewood, Jr., Eugene Clyde Brooks, EDUCATOR AND PUBLIC SERVANT, Preface.

[2] *Ibid.*, p. 114.

Our story of the Brooks' administration deals largely with the reforms which had a great influence upon the status of Negro education, viz., the stabilization of certificates, the adoption of a salary schedule, the resurgence of summer school attendance, the establishment of the Division of Negro Education, and the school building program.

Gatewood says that the major achievements of Brooks were: (1) the improvement of teachers; (2) the school building program; and (3) the advance in Negro education.

> Although the educational advantages of the Negro children remain strikingly inferior to those of the white children, nevertheless, he laid the foundation for a reputable system of Negro education that gradually materialized under his successors.[3]

Certification and Salary Schedules

None of these reforms were more important than those of certification and teachers' salary schedules. Payment for service rendered is inevitably linked with the quality of that service. Some uniformity in paying teachers had long existed and the criterion for salary paid was based upon some form of certificate — usually obtained by examination: Obviously educational achievement had some influence upon acquiring a certificate. The fact that local examiners and superintendents could issue certificates permitting sufficient leeway by which inefficient teachers were often assigned to positions in the schools.

The task of Brooks in getting his program of certification and salary scheduling established was facilitated by the adoption of the report of the State Educational Commission created by the General Assembly in 1917 to make a thorough study of educational conditions in North Carolina.

The survey was completed in 1920 and was submitted to the General Assembly in 1921. It set forth recommendations as to the relationship of the State Administration with that of the cities and counties; the training of teachers; the administering of public funds; and publicity and statistics.

The General Assembly adopted in the main the recommendations of the Commission and placed the public school system under the control of the State Department of Public Instruction.[4]

Brooks' main objective in establishing his program of certification and salary scheduling was the training of teachers in order that they might merit better pay. It was the first great stride, racewise, toward equalization of teachers' salaries.

---

[3] *Ibid.*, pp. 151, 152.

[4] Introduction, REPORT OF STATE EDUCATIONAL COMMISSION OF N. C.: Public Education in North Carolina; General Education Board, 61 Broadway, New York, pp. IX, XIV.

With an appropriation of $50,000, Brooks instituted the most comprehensive program of teacher training the State had ever known. With the incomparable A. T. Allen as Director of Teacher Training, the State was divided into districts and each member of the State Board of Education was assigned to a district for the purpose of supervising the summer teacher training program in the counties within his district. It motivated a great awakening of teacher training in summer schools with the salary schedule being a main incentive.[5]

A great boost to the Negro schools came in 1921 when the General Assembly created the Division of Negro Education with Newbold as Director. This Act was to give better supervision to Negro education and to offset the long neglect experienced by schools for colored children.

Newbold worked closely with Brooks in implementing the new programs among Negro schools. Mrs. Annie W. Holland, who had been one of the first Jeanes supervisors, was made Elementary Supervisor and W. A. Robinson, who had been a high school teacher in Louisville, Kentucky, was appointed high school inspector. An annual appropriation of $12,500 was made for the Negro Division which also had supervision over Indian schools[6].

Status of Training in 1919-20

In order to understand the condition relative to the training of teachers with the resurgence of education under Brooks, let us look at some simple statistics. Of the 12,622 white teachers and principals in 1919-20, only 2,549 or 20 percent held professional certificates; while only 245 of the 3,690 colored teachers, or 7 per cent held such certificates. Detailed information of preparation and experience was procured from 9,800 of 11,712 white and from 2,357 of 3,251 colored teachers in 1918-19. A tabulation of the status of training among colored teachers follows:

TABLE I

Institution	Attending	Attending & Graduating	Total
Public Elementary Only	406	0	406
County Training School	10	7	17
State Training School	197	148	345
Private School	667	648	1,315
School Out of State	134	140	274
Total	1,414	943	2,357

From these data it appears 17 per cent of colored teachers had not gone further than the elementary school.[7]

---

[5] Gatewood, *Op. Cit.*, p. 123.

[6] Biennial Report 1920-22, p. 34.

[7] Report of State Educational Commission., *Op. cit.*, p. 41.

Endeavoring to correct this pitable status, A. T. Allen, who had been placed in charge of the normal schools, began at once to standardize them.

In these schools some normal training was given in the last two years of the course, but most of the work done was in the regular high school curriculum and two thirds of the enrollment was in the practice schools. In the first three grades there were local children, but students in the fourth grade and above and who came from a distance were often admitted. More than half of the pupils at Elizabeth City and at Fayetteville were in the 6th and 7th grades and came from a distance. At Slater Normal the proportion was not so great as there were better elementary schools in Winston-Salem.

Allen further noted that there was no training for colored youth at public expense above the secondary level and that it was incumbent upon the State to provide for the training of principals.

Allen's report on the attendance at the normal schools is shown in Table II.[8]

TABLE II

1919-1920

	7th Grade and Below	Above 7th Grade	Total	Graduates
Fayetteville State Normal	245	104	349	
Elizabeth City State Normal	200	114	314	
Slater Normal, Winston	348	162	510	
1919-1920				
Fayetteville	360	142	502	6
Elizabeth City	374	176	550	17
Slater (Winston)	194	178	123	23

Training and Certification

To Allen, the training of teachers and certification went hand in hand — training being adopted as a basis for issuing certificates, designated as: primary, grammar grade, and high school; with A, B, and C classification in each. The trend in issuing certificates was shown by using an index of training of teachers.

In 1921-22, 68.26% of white teachers had an index varying from 354.5 to 718.5. The next year 68.26% of white teachers came within the limits of training which varied from 378.5 to 734.5. The coefficients of variation indicated 6% less variation in training of white teachers in 1922-23 than in 1921-22.

For the first year of the Biennium, two-thirds of Negro teachers had an index of training which varied from 252.5 to 544.4. After one

---

[8] Biennial Report, 1920-22, Report on Colored Normal Schools, p. 6.

year of functioning of the Division of Certification, the index of training of Negro teachers ranged from 339.5 to 633.5. The coefficients of variation for the last two years were 36.64 and 30.21 respectively. The relationship between the two coefficients showed 18 per cent less variation in training of Negro teachers in 1922-23 than in 1921-22. The Division of Certification tended to raise the index of all teachers.[9]

From these data on Table II, supplementing those of Table I, it appears that 17 per cent of colored teachers had not gone further than elementary school and 43 per cent probably had more than an elementary schooling, but less than high school; and 35 per cent had probably the equivalent of a high school education and 5 per cent were graduates of schools claiming college rank. Six reported having graduated from A&T College, thirteen from Biddle University, seventy-three from Shaw University, two from Fisk University, fifteen from Hampton Institute, two from Howard University, and three from Tuskegee Institute.[10]

Comparable figures on the status of white teachers are not given, but data from the State Educational Commission indicate that 59 per cent of white high school teachers had 4 years in college or more, but 78 were graduates of non-standard colleges.

The First Salary Schedule

With all the necessary data that he seemed to need, Brooks now proceeded to set his program of salary scheduling into action. The County School Budget Act of 1919 required preparation in May of an annual budget showing the number of schools, enrollment, average daily attendance, and the number of teachers with class and grade of certificate held. The budget was to form the basis for levying taxes the following year. To allow for unforseen changes in enrollment and consequent increase in number of teachers after the opening of school, the budget would be amended in November. On this basis the State would apportion its funds for three months. The number of teachers would be determined by the average daily attendance and salaries by class and grade of certificate held.

As a result of this Act, all teachers for the first time were certified in 1919-20; and for the first time the State was informed as to the standing of teachers holding each kind of certificate.

Table III shows the number of teachers by race holding the various classes of certificates:

TABLE III

	White Teachers	Colored Teachers
1. Second Grade	3,451	2,375

---

[9] Report, Educational Commission, *Op. cit.*, p. 13.

[10] *Ibid.*, pp. 42, 43, 44.

2. Provisional B	98	41
3. Provisional A	355	15
4. Temporary	1,708	328
5. Elementary	4,461	686
6. High and Special	2,197	213
7. Principal	352	32
Total	12,622	3,690

The results showed that 44 per cent of the white teachers and 75 per cent of the Negro teachers were below State standard.[11]

TABLE IV — SALARY SCHEDULE

Second Grade Certificates ....$ 45.00
Provisional B 50.00
Provisional A 55.00
Temporary 60.00

	No Experience	1 Yr.	2 Yrs.	3 Yrs.	4 Yrs.
Elementary:					
No College Training	$ 65.00	$ 70.00	$ 75.00	$ 80.00	$ 85.00
Equiv. 1 yr. College	75.00	80.00	85.00	90.00	95.00
Higher Certificates Primary, Grammar Grade and High School Based on 2 Years College or Examination	85.00	90.00	95.00	100.00	105.00
Grad. Norm. or 3 stn. College	90.00	95.00	100.00	105.00	110.00
Graduate of a College	100.00	105.00	110.00	120.00	133.33

Brooks' comments on his first salary schedule follows:

The raise in salary is based on the raise in certificate. The salary provided is the same as that paid in 1919-20. The maximum allowed for the best qualified teacher after 4 years is $133.33 for nine months. This is about the salary of a good stenographer. To reach this salary a teacher must attend summer school for 6 weeks at his own expense.

The first salary schedule did not indicate the status of salaries of Negro teachers, but they were as a rule paid below the scale. However, Brooks' revised schedule included a definite scale for Negro teachers. It further indicated five steps from "no experience" to that of "4 years experience" in the three levels of training. In all categories a minimum number of professional credits was required. While the scale of salaries for Negro teachers was lower than that for white teachers, it tended to lessen the differential between salaries of Negro

---

[11] S. P. I. Correspondence, File Box 76.

and white teachers and paved the way for a complete abolition of such differentials.[12]

TABLE V

Graduate Salary Scale for White Teachers

	Monthly Salary Based on Service				
	4 Yrs.	3 Yrs.	2 Yrs	1 Yr.	0
High School, Grammar Grade and Primary Certificates					
Class A — Graduate of A Standard A-Grade College with 18 Semester Hours in Professional Work	$133.33	$120.00	$110.00	$105.00	$100.00
Class B — Completion of 3 Yrs. of Standard College or 2 Yrs of Normal School with 12 Semester Hours in Professional Work	110.00	105.00	100.00	95.00	90.00
Class C — 2 Years of Standard College with 6 Semester Hours in Professional Work	105.00	100.00	95.00	90.00	85.00
Provisional Class C	95.00	90.00	85.00	80.00	75.00
Elementary Teachers Certificates					
Class A — One Year of Standard College or Normal School	95.00	90.00	85.00	80.00	75.00
Class B — Graduation From Standard High School and One Unit of Summer School Work	85.00	80.00	75.00	70.00	65.00
Provisional Elementary	75.00	70.00	65.00	60.00	55.00
Certificates Below Standard Temporary — 3 Years of High School and One Unit of County Summer School Work				60.00	
Provisional A — 2 Years of High School				55.00	
Provisional B — One Year of High School				50.00	
County Second Grade				45.00	

(*See footnote following Graduated Salary Scale for Negro Teachers)

---

[12] Rules and Other Information, November Budget and Apportionment Public School Funds, S. P. I. Correspondence, pp. 7, 8.

TABLE VI

Graduated Salary Schedule for Negro Teachers

Monthly Salary Based on Length of Service

	4 Yrs.	3 Yrs.	2 Yrs	1 Yr.	0
High School, Grammar Grade and Primary Certificates					
Class A — Graduate of a Standard A-Grade College with 18 Semester Hours Professional Work	$100.00	$ 95.00	$ 90.00	$ 85.00	$ 80.00
Class B — Three Years Standard College or 2 Years Normal with 12 Semester Hours Professional Credit	90.00	85.00	80.00	75.00	70.00
Class C — Two Years Standard College with 6 Semester Hours Professional Credit	80.00	77.50	75.00	72.50	70.00
Provisional Class C	75.00	70.00	65.00	60.00	57.50
Elementary Teachers Certificates					
Class A — One Year Standard College or Normal School	75.00	70.00	65.00	60.00	57.50
Class B — Graduation From A Standard High School and One Unit of Summer School Work	70.00	65.00	60.00	57.50	55.00
Provisional Elementary	65.00	60.00	55.00	52.50	50.00
Certificates Below Standard					
Temporary — 3 Years High School and One Unit of County Summer School Work				55.00	
Provisional A — 2 Years High School Work				50.00	
Provisional B — One Year of High School Work				47.50	
County Second Grade				35.00	45.00
County Third Grade				35.00	

(*Both scales taken from Document: Rules and Other Information concerning November Budget and Apportionment of Public School Funds; SPI Correspondence, pp. 7, 8, File Box 76)

Negro Division of Education

We now turn our attention to what is the most outstanding contribution of E. C. Brooks toward the education of Negroes in the

State. Of the many reforms and innovations of the Brooks' regime, none was more helpful to Negroes than the establishment of the Division of Negro Education; and no individual connected with the Division was more genuinely loved than its director, N. C. Newbold.

Speaking in advocacy of his proposal to set up such a division, Brooks said:

> One of the greatest needs of the State, perhaps, is a Division of Negro Education with one man in charge who shall have a general supervision over all Negro education in the State. Any one acquainted with conditions knows that educational opportunities for Negroes are not what they should be.[13]

The Division of Negro Education, created in 1921, was given an annual appropriation of $15,000. At the outset it contained a staff of nine persons, white and Negro — a group larger than the entire Department of Public Instruction a decade earlier.[14]

Negroes working in the Division under Newbold and G. H. Ferguson, Assistant Director, were W. A. Robinson, High School Inspector, Mrs. Annie W. Holland, Elementary Schools Supervisor, Mrs. Florence Williams, Health Coordinator who was borrowed from the State Board of Health, and Dr. G. E. Davis, Agent for the Rosenwald Fund.

The writer points with pride to his relationships with Newbold and his efficient staff of workers. No meeting of State proportions was ever complete without the appearance of N. C. Newbold. He would even go far into the backward places to talk with the common people — farmers, ministers, teachers, and business people anywhere in the State. Many important conferences were convoked by Newbold and Brooks to inspire Negroes with a zeal to improve their new opportunities. Theirs was the "Campaign for Education" all over again.

There were the wonderful women like Miss Susan Fulghum, Miss Hattie Parrot and Miss Mary Bell Delmar who painstakingly aided the leaders in understanding the new programs of Certification and summer school objectives. There were men like A. T. Allen, Director of Teacher Training; J. Henry Highsmith, Inspector of high schools; prominent Negro leaders: clergymen, like Bishops Clement and Walls; businessmen like Berry O'Kelly; and heads of institutions like Atkins, Smith, Moore, and James E. Shepard, all of whom willingly cooperated with Newblod to infuse new life into Negro education.

In the rural districts, with the aid of the Rosenwald School Building program, improved buildings sprang up all over the State. With the aid of the Slater Fund, county training schools were in-

---

[13] S. P. I. Correspondence, undated document; File Box 76.

[14] Gatewood, *Op. cit.*, p. 168.

creasing. And with the aid of the Jeanes Fund, supervision of rural schools was improving the quality of teaching and learning. Finally, in cooperation with farm and home demonstration agents, Negro people in general were enjoying a new birth of educational progress.

Although Brooks was never over-shadowed in his leadership, it was Newbold who carried the torch, lighting the path to progress. He induced the General Education Board to appropriate funds to train principals for high schools. He made arrangements with Hampton Institute to include special training in its summer schools for prospective high school principals. He secured grants from the General Education Board to establish teacher training courses in certain institutions of the State.

Perhaps Newbold's greatest act of educational statesmanship came in 1925 when he induced the denominational secondary institutions to turn their schools over to the State in the wake of standardization with which private schools could not compete.[15]

Brooks' School Building Program

We return now to another phase of the Brooks Administration, the School Building program which represents another of his remarkable achievements. With due credit to the long Joyner regime in keeping opposition to Negro education at a minimum, it must be recognized that little progress in school building for Negroes was made under his administration. Without the aid of the General Education Board, The Rosenwald Fund, the Jeanes Fund, and the Slater Board, Negro schools indeed would have been a disgrace to the State.

Brooks sensed the enormities of the problem and endeavored to gain sympathetic consideration by whites as well as the faith of Negro leaders. In addition he sought the favor of the philanthropic agencies which had already been aiding Negro schools and used his skill and diplomacy in presenting the question to the General Assembly.

Conferences with Negro leaders were held in February and in April of 1919 at Winston-Salem. Their main purpose was to assure Negroes that Brooks was sincere in his efforts to improve Negro education. In a letter to Dr. James E. Shepard, he said:

> We are planning many improvements in teacher training, high school instruction, erection of school houses, and other educational needs of colored people . . . I think it would be wise for you and your committee to be considering some platform that both white and colored people might stand on that would be of mutual interest to all concerned.

Accepting this proffer of good will, Negro leaders met at Brooks' call on September 20, 1919, and adopted a "Declaration of Principles" as a guide in creating an "unprecedented era of good feeling" between

---

[15] Brown, A HISTORY OF EDUCATION OF NEGROES IN N. C., pp. 49, 6b.

the races. The declaration condemned lynching and all other forms of injustice, intermingling of the races on a social basis and urged Negroes to have faith that the "white man is ready to help."[16]

The document was widely circulated within the State and in other states. Dr. Francis H. Rose of Virginia Union University, Richmond, Virginia, in congratulating Brooks, wrote for copies to distribute. He said:

> I find that the colored students in our schools most heartily endorse it and it seems to meet with approval of both white and colored people all over the country.[17]

The "era of good feeling" motivated Brooks to prove the "faith in the white man" set forth in the Declaration of Principles. He had already persuaded the Legislature of 1919 to appropriate $90,000 for permanent improvements at the three normal schools and to increase their maintenance fund to $35,000. He now proposed to establish a high school for Negroes in every county.

A letter from United States Commissioner of Education, P. P. Claxton to Brooks on August 17, 1920, inquired if it were true that he (Brooks) intended to establish a Negro high school in every county. . . . "If true, I am delighted," said Claxton. Brooks replied on August 19, 1920:

> I have stated to the County Superintendents in every meeting that we have held so far that it is absolutely necessary to provide at least one high school for (n)egroes in every county where there is a considerable number of (n)egroes.[18]

Brooks was equally insistent upon making the normal schools a real credit to the State by improving their physical potentialities. He therefore persuaded the Legislature of 1921 to appropriate $400,000 for buildings and equipment for the normals. In addition he secured $10,000 from the General Education Board, $2,000 from the Rosenwald Fund, and a contribution of $2,510 from the Negroes themselves.

A Legislative Act of 1921 placed the State Normals under the State Board of Education and, with another large contribution from the General Education Board in 1922, Brooks was able to convert these institutions into real normal schools with facilities adequate to prepare teachers for higher grade certificates.[19]

Our story here omits the activities of Brooks relative to the building of schools for white children as it was explained in the introduc-

---

[16] Gatewood, Op. cit., pp. 163ff.

[17] S. P. I. Correspondence, Letter from Francis Rose, Virginia Union University, September 26, 1919.

[18] S. P. I. Correspondence; P. P. Claxton to E. C. Brooks; reply to P. P. Claxton.

[19] Gatewood, Op. cit., p. 168.

tion that this story would be beamed toward the education of Negro schools, but through the Division of School House Planning created in his department, there was a resurgence in school building for both races.

One of the greatest experiences of this writer was the honor of being associated as an instructor in summer schools with some of the leading educators in the State as well as to have been intimately associated with Newbold and Brooks. In addition it was an experience worth remembering to have listened to some of the representatives of the great funds which aided Negro education like James Hardy Dillard and Jackson Davis of the Jeanes and Slater Boards. Indeed the writer owes much of his educational enhancement as a recipient of one of those educational grants of the General Education Board.

As the story approaches the close of the Brooks regime, let us note the status of those great institutions, the normal schools, which had been a great bulwark of the teacher training program since their inception.

All the State Normals (including Durham State Normal, 1923, formerly National Training School; now North Carolina College) and A. and T. College regularly conducted summer schools. A. and T. College by far had the largest attendance. It was directed by F. D. Bluford who became President of the College upon the death of J. B. Dudley. In addition to the State (or approved) summer schools, many counties or combination of counties conducted summer schools for those teachers with certificates below State standards; Primary, Grammar Grade, and High School. Holders of these were required to attend State or approved summer schools.

While the story of this great awakening in teacher training has included its impact upon Negro education, it could equally chronicle that among white teachers as the same type of program emanated from the State Supervisor of Teacher Training of the State Department of Public Instruction and applied alike to all teachers of the State; only the salary scale was different and, at this state of educational history, they were all in separate schools.

While this renaissance in teacher improvement ensued, local school management, city and county, was attracted by the contagion of educational resurgence and handsome brick school buildings were erected in many cities and towns while cooperation of county management with certain of the philanthropic agencies, eliminated many of the one and two teacher schools with more commodious school buildings known as Rosenwald schools. In 1923 there were 300 Rosenwald schools in the State. In addition, county training schools, aided by the Slater Fund, were established in many counties.[20]

The success of Brooks as a school building State Superintendent was largely the result of the many years of educating the public in favor of education — a task which earlier State Superintendents were

---

[20] Brown, *Op. cit.*, p. 58.

never able to accomplish. This resurgence under Brooks really had its beginning in the Campaign for Universal Education, under Aycock as Governor. Brooks had at his command that which nearly every one of his predecessors craved — funds to operate and to build. The State Loan Fund of $10,000,000, created largely through his influence, was a tremendous stimulus to the building of school houses, while his creation of the Division of School House planning insured economy in construction and in placement.

Consolidation of schools was a natural concomitant of school placement and, under Brooks' policy, 756 districts were abolished between 1919 and 1923. In the same period, schools with four or more teachers more than doubled and one teacher schools decreased from 4,437 to 3, 240.[21]

Among the Negro rural schools in 1915 there were 1,934 one-teacher schools or 80%. In 1924-25, the number had been reduced to 1,263 or 52%.[22]

The record of Brooks' administration is an epic of a "Golden Age" in Negro education, but the whole story cannot be told fully here. Suffice it to say that he was a power of accomplishment and a disciple for fairness and justice. Some educators feared him; all respected him. His fiery oratory was convincing and usually hit its mark. He surrounded himself with able men; trusted them and permitted ample freedom of operation by them. Negro leaders specifically loved him and had faith in him. Under no State Superintendent had they experienced such progress for, like a gladiator, fearless and determined, he used his great skill and talent for the promotion of a cause, as he saw it, for right and justice in the education of all the children of the State.

---

[21] Gatewood, *Op. cit.*, pp. 151, 156.

[22] Brown, *Op. cit.*, p. 55.

Chapter IX

The Administration of A. T. Allen
1923-34

As a disciple of E. C. Brooks, Arch T. Allen was thoroughly immersed in the Brooks' philosophy of renovating the State's educational system. In fact, as Director of Teacher Training, he had been the chief architect in the certification and training program which so remarkably characterized the Brooks' regime. The foundation had been well laid; Allen had only to build thereon.

That he was thoroughly equal to the task, no one had a serious doubt as he entered upon his duties with a firm resolution to move the State ahead in its responsibility to the children of the schools. He was keenly aware of the conditions among Negro schools in general and of the inequities of rural education in particular. The 6-Month's term had persisted since the days of Joyner, and although consolidation and transportation had been started, the opportunities of rural children were far inferior to those afforded children in the cities and towns.

The aim in this Chapter is to set forth for the reader four important phases of Allen's administration which tended to have an impact upon the Negro schools: (1) the trend toward equality in rural schools and elementary school standardization; (2) progress in salary increases, length of term and consolidation of districts; (3) Negro Education with the collaboration of Newbold in Normal school development; and (4) a brief sketch of the Negro leadership personalities of the period.

In his prospect to secure longer school terms in the rural districts, Allen moved with challenging objectivity in promulgating a standardization scheme which he felt would greatly motivate local initiative of equal terms with towns and cities.

The elementary school, Allen noted, was the most neglected area of education. It was almost impossible to secure efficient, competent teachers to work in a system of only six months. There was often a feeling, even among some educational leaders, that "most anybody" could teach an elementary school, especially if it was a "country school." The single salary schedule, placing all teaching positions on the same level had served to increase respect for elementary teaching. Standard elementary requirement of facilities would further awaken sentiment for an increased school term in the rural schools. With standardization there would no longer be a feeling that teaching in the upper grades was more honorable than teaching in the lower grades.

Criteria for standardizing elementary schools were adopted to include the following:

1. A seven-year course of study
2. A term of 8 months (or 160 days exclusive of holidays)
3. At least 7 full time teachers
4. Qualifications — At least the Elementary A Certificate
5. Attendance at least 205 in average daily attendance
6. Requirements for completion of a standard elementary school must include a satisfactory completion of prescribed course
7. A 7-year course in general elementary subjects
8. Equipment
   a. At least 3 sets of supplementary readers: 20 copies in each
   b. A library of 300 volumes
   c. Special equipment for primary work

The proposal had no immediate wide-spread effect upon rural schools, as far as extended terms were concerned, but it did activate interest in standardizing elementary schools generally. It was not a legal requirement, but was made to stimulate rural school advancement.

Allen also called attention to wide differences in daily cost of elementary and of high school administration; the number of pupils per teacher in each; the average monthly salaries and indices of scholarship of teachers. The following is Allen's appraisal of these inequities:

TABLE I

		Elementary	High School
A.	*Daily Cost*		
	State As A Whole	.181	.392
	Rural Schools Only	.172	.400
	City Schools Only	.211	.383
B.	*Number of Pupils Per Teacher*		
	State As A Whole	25.7	20.4
	Rural Schools Only	24.7	18.4
	City Schools Only	29.6	21.0
C.	*Average Monthly Salary*		
	State As A Whole	$ 93.27	$ 155.05
	Rural Schools Only	85.12	147.26
	City Schools Only	125.01	160.98
D.	*Index of Scholarship*		
	State As A Whole	470.1	745.7
	Rural Schools Only	443.4	735.7
	City Schools Only	635.4	759.1

According to Allen's interpretation of the average daily cost of the schools, the State was spending 116 per cent more to teach one high school pupil one day than it was spending to teach one elementary pupil one day. In the rural schools the difference was 132 per cent while the gap in the cities' effort was only 81 per cent. The number of pupils per teacher, difference in salaries, and the differences in scholarship all operated against the status of elementary teaching in both rural and in city schools.[1]

General School Progress

Despite the inequities noted above, it is evident that a momentum of progress in public schools was increasing. In 1922-23 the average monthly salary of white teachers was $107.14; that of the Negro teachers $63.94. In 1923-24, the white teachers' average was $109.40, an increase of $2.26 while the Negro teachers' was $64.83 or an increase of $0.89.* The average length of term in 1922-23 was 143.9 days among white schools; 132.6 days among Negro schools. In 1923-24, the white average was 146.2; Negro, 134.6. Total value of school property rose from $24 million in 1920 to $60 million in 1924.[2]

Progress in rural education is shown in the movement toward consolidation and its natural concomitant, transportation. In 1923-24 there were 634 white and 57 colored districts consolidated.

TABLE II

	White	Colored
Number of Schools Having 4 Teachers	130	32
Number of Schools Having 5 Teachers	85	12
Number of Schools Having 6 Teachers	16	7
Number of Schools Having More Than 6	343	6
Number of Districts Abolished	279	37
Number of Trucks (Buses) Not Listed by Race	1,318	
Number of Pupils Transported	45,251[3]	

Although Allen's report specifies neither the number of trucks (buses) transporting Negro children nor the number transported, we do know that some Negro children were being transported to schools in many districts of the State during the term, 1923-24.

Superintendent Allen was no less an advocate of improved Negro education than was his predecessor, E. C. Brooks. As Director of Teacher Training under Brooks, he had immediate supervision of the Normal Schools and wanted to see them developed into real Normals. In order to raise their standards, he advocated more high schools for Negro children. As high school graduates would increase,

---

[1] Biennial Report 1922-24, p. 25.

* Actually, the per cent of Negro salaries was 4 points lower in 1923-24 than in 1922-23.

[2] *Ibid.*, Part II, p. 198.

[3] *Ibid.*, p. 235; Table XIX.

he said, high school students in the Normals would decrease, and consequently Normal students would increase. Entrance to the Normal schools and other higher institutions, therefore, would be based upon graduation from standard high schools. Before graduating from a Colored Normal school, a student had to meet requirements as rigid as those in any Normal in the State. The colored Normals were working on the most vital question of Negro education — finding efficient teachers for the lower grades where the great number of colored children seemed hopelessly lodged.[4]

Both Newbold and Allen were thoroughly acquainted with the situation with regard to the status of the Normal schools and their relationship with high school training. Most of the Negro high schools went no further than the 10th Grade and sent their graduates to the Normals or to the colleges for the fourth year of high school. Newbold's plan was to induce the private higher institutions to abolish their academies and the Normal schools to raise their entrance requirement so that public high schools could assume the responsibility of standardizing their schools.

In addition to his far fetched plan of high school growth, Newbold advocated additional Normal Schools to meet the increasing demand for efficiently trained teachers. Durham Normal (The National Training School at Durham) became the 4th Normal school in 1923. With funds he secured from the General Education Board, Newbold induced 15 of the State's private higher and secondary institutions to establish special teacher training courses to aid the State to meet the demand for teachers. Although this arrangement was only temporary, it served to supplement the arduous task of the Normal schools in supplying the great need of competent teachers.[5]

In these colleges and secondary institutions, students in the 4th year of high school pursued intensive courses of professional work along with their regular high school courses. Newbold secured experienced special teacher training instructors to aid them and at the conclusion of their courses, including 18 hours of professional credits, they were able to qualify for a standard State certificate. Many teachers left their positions temporarily to take advantage of this provision and to merit higher pay.

On the subject of Negro education, Allen included in the introduction of his Biennial Report of 1922-1924 the following:

> There seems to be a disposition to concede to the Negro an education far more adequate than he has heretofore enjoyed. Negroes are accepting the privilege of going to school in good faith and are availing themselves of the opportunity in a most commendable manner. The opportunity of a colored child to get an education is nowhere equal to the op-

---

[4] *Ibid.*, p. 41.

[5] Brown, *Op. Cit.*, p. 59; Table p. 60

portunity afforded the white child, but the gap is being narrowed as colored schools are improved.[6]

Allen pointed out that the trend in Negro Education was upward. Outstanding in this trend was that of the Rosenwald School Building program. In 1925-26, the Fund provided 245 classrooms at a total cost of $478,157 of which Negroes themselves contributed $59,622; white friends, $1,750; the Rosenwald Fund, $69,800; and the public funds, $346,945. Prior to 1921, the total cost of Rosenwald schools amount to $2,797,210 of which $1,775,534 had come from public funds.[7]

Practically all this growth — The Rosenwald Program — was reflected in rural and in elementary education, but under the dynamic activities of J. Henry Highsmith, Inspector of High Schools, and W. A. Robinson, State Supervisor of Negro High Schools, a resurgence in high school emphasis, both in buildings and in standardization, began to assert itself. The erection of durable brick structures for Negro high schools had begun before Allen's time, but the momentum increased under his administration with the master-minding diplomacy of Newbold. A letter written February 20, 1923, by Newbold to Superintendent K. R. Curtis of Kinston, urging him to build a much needed structure for Negroes is an indication of the strategy used by Newbold to motivate the building of Negro high schools:

> ... Washington is planning to build a Negro school costing $70,000. Goldsboro is also planning a new construction and New Bern has two very nice brick buildings.*[8]

For the high school future, Newbold recommended the appointment of a supervisor of the county training schools which he said were our only hope for standard high schools in the rural districts.[9]

In 1922-23 there were only 8 accredited Negro high schools in the State. There were 79 teachers and 1,448 pupils enrolled. There were 72 graduates in that year. In 1925-26, the number of Negro high schools accredited was 72, with 303 teachers and 8,237 pupils enrolled. The number of graduates reached 752.[10]

As the writer was a part of this resurgence in high school development, he can speak with authority as to much of the activity

---

[6] Biennial Report 1922-24, p.38.

[7] Biennial Report 1924-26, Chapter 6, p. 65.

[8] Letter from Newbold to H. R. Curtis, Sup't Kinston; February 2, 1923 SPI Corr. File Box 6.

* Actually the Goldsboro structure included 3 buildings; a high school and 2 elementary opened early in 1924.

[9] Letter from Newbold to Brooks February 20, 1923; SPI Corr. File Box 6

[10] Biennial Report 1924-26; Chapter 6, p. 67.

among Negro school men to meet the challenges of high school standardization. Many of the Negro high schools were graduating students at the end of the 10th Grade (Third year of high school at that time) thus forcing them to go to the college academies or to Normal schools to secure their 4th year of high school.

In 1924 the writer had just begun his principalship of the "Colored" (the original Dillard) High School in Goldsboro. With approval of the Trustees of the Goldsboro Graded Schools and the Superintendent, O. A. Hamilton, he informed the expectant Class of 1925 that, for the purposes of standardization there would be no graduation that year, but students would be held over for the 11th Grade.* The announcement virtually precipitated a "strike," but every pupil except one returned for the 11th Grade.

This brief account of a pattern followed by most of the Negro high schools is a preliminary to the story of a forward movement in the development of the State Normals.

Newbold and The State Normals

The reader will recall that under the administrations of Mebane and Joyner the trend was to decrease the number of state Normal schools. They were actually reduced under Joyner from 8 to 3. During the educational resurgence of Brooks, Allen, and Newbold the tendency was to reverse the previous policy. Newbold advocated an increase from the three, which survived the Joyner curtailment, to five which he felt needed to meet the rapidly increasing demand for trained teachers. He finally settled for four. Writing to Allen on June 26, 1923, he said:

> This year for the first time in their history, classes were graduated from the normal courses which means 2 years above high school . . . next year probably 50 will be be graduated and after that the number will be fairly rapidly increased. Should we establish and develop 2 more normals, making 5 altogether and graduate 50 from normals, this would mean 250 properly trained new teachers to go into the State's Negro public schools.[11]

From the writer's recollection, bolstered by the record, comes an interesting story involving Newbold and one of the most colorful and able of the Negro educators of the period. It is the story of a controversy between Newbold and James E. Shepard, head of the National Training School at Durham.

In as much as the story had a happy ending which greatly enhanced the status of Negro education in the State, it is not without place in this picture.

---

* The system over the State was a "7-4 grade instead of an 8-4."

[11] Letter from Newbold to Allen, June 26, 1923; File Box 6; SPI Corr.

DR. JAMES E. SHEPARD

Founder, North Carolina College, Durham

Shepard was an able administrator and an ambitious personality. He had dreamed of being a president of a college and had founded an institution in 1910 which he called, National Religious Training School and Chatauqua, with the objective to develop young men and young women of fine character and sound academic training requisite for real service to the Nation. But his institution ran into financial difficulties, was sold in 1915 and changed its name to National Training School with Shepard still as its head. Finally in 1923, it was turned over to the State as the 4th of the State Normal schools.

Here the controversy between Newbold and Shepard began. Shepard persisted in trying to fulfill his dream of being a college president and offered certain college courses. Newbold insisted that the courses be strictly kept within the scope of the Normal curriculum. Numerous letters passed between the two. Shepard, always the astute politician that he was, diplomatically and graciously condescended to Newbold's requests.

In the midst of the controversy, Newbold disclosed a proposal which had long been in the back of his mind — a four year teachers college for Negroes. On July 18, 1925, Newbold wrote to Allen recommending Slater State Normal at Winston-Salem to become a 4-year teachers college:

> At present there is no state institution in which we may train high school principals and teachers for Negro schools. The Mayor and city officials of Winston-Salem, the City Superintendent and the Board of Trustees of the local schools and leading business men and women indorse the proposal made by the Board of Trustees.[12]

The indorsement of this proposal by Newbold, as far as Shepard was concerned, literally "threw the fat into the fire." The controversy waged hot, with sentiment about equally divided among Negro educators, Critics of Shepard's activities, enhancing the prestige of his own institution, might have been more sympathetic toward him had they better understood the far flung and long standing objectives of the man. He, himself, had been trained as a pharmacist. He had had great hopes of building a college which would eventually approach university status and train leaders in liberal arts and in the professions. In turning his institution over to the State, he had clung to the idea of an institution beyond the status of a Normal school.

Neither might his proponents have opposed Newbold's indorsement of Winston-Salem as a 4-year teachers college had they thoroughly understood the importance of the priority in training high school principals and teachers needed in the development of high schools.

Shepard was a man of great popular stature. He had for many years been President of the State Teachers Association and Grand

---

[12] Letter from Newbold to Allen, July 18, 1925; SPI Corr. File Box 6.

Master of the Masons. In addition, he held the ear of many prominent white citizens, some of whom were prominent in the Legislature.

The final solution of the controversy as to whether the 4-year teachers college should go to Winston-Salem or to Durham produced the greatest forward step in Negro education of the Brooks, Allen, and Newbold era. More far reaching than solving of the "Tale of the Two Cities" was its impact upon the other two Normals, Fayetteville and Elizabeth City, both of which were ultimately elevated to 4-year teachers colleges. Winston-Salem had its 4-year teachers college and Durham its liberal arts and professional college, thus bringing to a reality Shepard's dream of becoming a college president. Thus a quiet controversy between two giant leaders in Negro education was resolved to the satisfaction and ulitimate good of all concerned.

Closely connected with this story of Shepard and his relationship with Newbold is the story of three other great educators who were in the twilight of their illustrious careers: S. G. Atkins, E. E. Smith, and P. W. Moore, whose lives were highly dramatized in Newbold's "Five Great Negro Educators." Only a brief mention is recorded here.

Atkins, quiet and soft spoken, but convincing, was a most versatile leader. He had served as a teacher at Livingstone College; was Secretary of Education for the A. M. E. Zion Church; he had represented the denomination at three different Ecumenical Conferences: Twice at London and once at Toronto. He was founder of Slater Normal and Industrial Academy (now Winston-Salem Teachers College). He was an ardent advocate of thoroughness and an example of culture and refinement. He was one of the founders of the State Teachers Association and in the mid twenties served as its president.

Smith, tall, stately, and with an abundance of personal magnetism, was a diplomat, soldier, and educator all blended into a pleasant personality. Though Smith was not its founder, the history of Fayetteville State Normal (now Teachers College) is inextricably identified with the life of E. E. Smith. He twice left the institution: first to serve as United States Minister to Liberia and second, to serve as Adjutant of the Third North Carolina Regiment in the Spanish-American War. His accomplishments were many, but perhaps the most outstanding was the selection of his succesor, J. W. Seabrook.

P. W. Moore, who stood at the birth of his institution, Elizabeth City State Normal (now Teachers College), was one of the most condescending men of ability it has been this writer's honor to know. He always made his conferees feel at home and was ever ready to help in any problem involving those with whom he worked. For many years he divested himself of much of his pitable salary to help some student in financial straits. He had been an instructor at the old Plymouth State Normal and transformed this experience into building at Elizabeth City an institution the influence of which stretched over most of the eastern counties of the State and spread over into the State of Virginia. He is remembered by having two schools named in his honor: one, an elementary school in Duplin County, the other a high school in Elizabeth City.

Some of the other personalities of the Newbold era who highly dramatized the period deserve more than a passing notice. There was W. A. Robinson, Supervisor of High Schools — already mentioned, who greatly aided the standardization of high schools; Annie W. Holland who spearheaded the activities of elementary education; and G. E. Davis, the Rosenwald School Building agent, whose golden oratory motivated men and women of both races to meet the challenge made by the Rosenwald Fund to improve Negro schools. Then there was Florence Williams, actually in the employ of the State Board of Health, but "loaned" to the Division of Negro Education to help dramatize the importance of health and sanitation and proper dieting. Mrs. Williams was a nurse who had thrilled thousands of soldiers overseas during the war with her dynamic personality and addresses on health. In the rural districts and at the summer schools in North Carolina she literally "preached the gospel" of proper dieting. She urged families to grow and eat all types of vegetables whether or not they liked them. "I don't like okra," she said, "but I just put it into my mouth close my eyes, and just let it slide on down." Mabel Carney, Professor of Rural Education, Teachers College, New York, well known to many teachers who attended Hampton Institute summer schools and Columbia University, wrote to Newbold about Mrs. Williams' activities at Columbia:

> I want to assure you that she made one of the best talks I have ever heard on health. Her organization and presentation of the topic were both excellent and it was a real joy to see the masterly way in which she handled the class. I consider her one of the finest women I have ever met of any race or hue.[13]

Newbold responded to Mrs. Carney:

> Mrs. Williams is a very capable, ambitious woman. She has been very serviceable to the State Board of Health and to the general cause of bettering the cause of the Negro people.[14]

Approaching the close of Allen's administration, we note among his accomplishments, the expanding of special areas of education which undoubtedly would influence the impact of Quality Education of a later period. The Vocational Agricultural program in 1925-26 showed 111 schools with a total enrollment of 3,377 pupils teaching vocational agriculture; Vocational Home Economics in 147 schools enrolling 6,261 pupils; and Vocational Trade education in 6 schools enrolling 125 pupils. The Smith-Sears Act of 1920 had enabled the State to locate and retrain 419 cripples for rehabilitation.[15]

---

[13] Letter from Mabel Carney to Newbold, May 11, 1923; SPI Corr. File Box 6.

[14] Reply from Newbold to Mabel Carney; SPI Corr. File Box 6.

[15] Biennial Report 1924-25; Chapter VII, p. 71.

The Congress of Colored Parents and Teachers, organized under the leadership of Mrs. Annie W. Holland in 1927 had a membership of 10,770 and raised that year $65,513.97. Two years later its convention had 953 delegates and reported a membership of 17,579. In 1931 there were 1,061 delegates and a total membership of 20,634. Four district associations were established in 1931.

The 8-months term, for which Allen had so earnestly advocated from the very beginning of his administration came in 1933, just one year before death put an end to his notable career as State Superintendent. He died October 20, 1934.

Under Allen, Negro education had been given remarkable advantages, rural education had been improved with consolidation, transportation and the final lengthening of the term. The high schools had been improved and many had been standardized. The Normals had all been made Teachers Colleges and the quality of teaching had been greatly improved. Allen had truly erected an endurable system upon the solid foundation of Brooks and his career in the State's educational history will be long remembered as one of the most progressive periods of Negro hope and advancement.

[16] Biennial Report 1930-32; Chapter 2; p. 57.

Chapter X

The Administration of Clyde A. Erwin
1934-1952

With rare exception, North Carolina has been favored with able and prophetic men to serve as State Superintendent of Public Instruction. Always looking ahead for some next step to improve the schools, each entered upon his duties with resolution and hope — hope that for most of them faded into despair where funds to run the schools were concerned.

Brooks and Allen were about the first superintendents to be blessed with adequate funds to operate an efficient system. Their problem was mainly one of legislative persuasion and implementation.

Clyde A. Erwin, who succeeded Allen, might have enjoyed the financial affluence of his immediate predecessors had not the great depression of the thirties descended up the Nation, but no administration had been more replete with progressive educational innovations than that of Clyde Erwin.

Of course some of these movements had their inception under Allen or even under Brooks, but they rose to fruition under Erwin. The following are among the most important: the enriched curriculum, the adoption of free text books, the adoption of a retirement system, Teacher Tenure, and the Twelve-Year program. Another measure of importance to Negroes was the lessening of salary differentials and the final adoption of equal salaries for equal qualification. In addition to these topics, the story recounts some comparable statistics to show progress for the first half of the Century; the improvement of training, the expansion of vocational Education, the growth of high schools for Negroes, and the status of the higher institutions.

As an introduction to the progress and status of the schools as reported by Erwin the reader should be interested in a few dry statistics covering a span of more than sixty years. Their comparative value would be found in the gradual, though at times almost imperceptible, abridgement of the wide gap between the education of whites and that of Negroes.

In 1869-70 there were 243,463 white and 141,155 colored children (6 to 21). In 1935-36 there were 771-320 white and 340,765 colored. The number enrolled in school was not given, but the percent in 1869-70 for all children was 70 while in 1935-36 the percent was 85.5. Another comparison of white and colored children of 1923-24 and 1935-36 located in the first and in the seventh grades showed the following: 116,077 white and 90,645 colored children in the first grade in 1923-24; 93,024 white and 76,797 colored in the first grade in 1935-36. For these same years the figures for the seventh grade were: 43,460 white and 8,519 colored (1923-24) as against 52,683 white and 17,663 colored in 1935-36.

In terms of percentage, 21 per cent of the white children and 36 per cent of the colored children in 1923-24 were in the First Grade while in 1935-36 there were only 21 per cent of the white and 28.4 of the colored in the First Grade.

In high school (1923-24) the comparison showed 12.4 per cent of the white and 2.3 per cent of the colored attending high school while in 1935-36 there were 23.1 white and 10.9 colored children attending high school.

The number of children per teacher in the elementary school for 1925-26 was 34.5 white and 46.2 colored; while in 1935-36 the number was 38.7 white and 40.4 colored. For these same years the number of children per teacher in high school was 49 white and 22.6 colored in 1925-26 as against 33.6 white and 32.6 colored in 1935-36.

In average daily attendance of the elementary schools for 1925-26, the figures were: 26.4 white and 30.6 colored. In the high school 17.9 white and 9.7 colored (1925-26). For the term 1935-36, the elementary figures were: 33.5 white, 32.6 colored. The high school figures were 29.9 white and 31.6 colored in 1935-36.

Length of school terms between white and colored showed a remarkable abridgement of the gap from 1900 through 1936. In 1900, rural white schools had an average of 73.3 number of days; colored rural schools, 65.3. In the cities the white schools had an average of 170 days while the colored schools had an average of 160 days. In 1935-36, rural white schools had an average of 160.1 days; rural colored, 159 days. In the cities the average number of days for both races was the same.

Erwin concluded from these statistics that colored children had not had so good a record of attendance nor opportunity in length of terms, as had the white children, but that the gap between the races was rapidly being abridged.

Commenting upon the situation, Erwin wrote:

The State-wide provision for a term of 160 days has meant and will mean much in the quantity and QUALITY* of work done in the elementary school. It is true that education is a spiritual process, but it is true also that it is a temporal process and the proper time for training of children is the early years of life and more nearly the whole of a child's time should be devoted to distinctive and thorough-going training.[1]

---

[1] Biennial Report 1934-36; pp. 7, 28.

* The capitals, QUALITY, are the writer's.

124

Undaunted by the great depression of the early Thirties which saw salaries of white teachers reduced 34.9 per cent and those of Negro teachers 26.8 per cent, Erwin in 1936 recommended restoration of previous salaries, longer school terms, and increases in scholarship of teachers. In addition, he advocated the adoption of an enriched curriculum to heighten the quality of health teaching, recreation, and the stabilization of the athletic program of the schools.[2]

An interesting innovation in the biennial reports of Clyde Erwin is his use of illustrations (photographs) of many activities of the enriched curriculum with which his reports are replete. To his credit, many activities of Negro schools are included.

The enriched curriculum went beyond the benefits of children in the schools, and included training of adults — Adult Education — and rehabilitation of individuals who were handicapped. These adult programs, which had grown out of the throes of the depression, helped to reduce illiteracy and improved home and school cooperation, home management, health, education of the deaf, and the development of home crafts. In 1939 Legislature provided $30,000 for Adult Education.

The George Dean Act of 1937 provided training in Distributive Education — training of regular employed workers in distributive occupations and for high school seniors who desired to enter that field of occupations. Under Erwin, North Carolina became one of the first states to offer Guidance under a cooperative arrangement with the United States Office of Education. Library service provided training for student assistants under trained library teachers.[3]

The State System of Education

Although the State Department had for many years handed down various suggestions — almost directives — for their implementation into county and city systems, most of these directives remained permissive. The foundation for a "State System" of education had actually been in operation since 1933 and had proved generally satisfactory. The legislative battle hinged around "from what source" the funds were to be raised by which the State Department institutions and schools were to be operated. The appropriations for the schools had been set at $20,031,000 for the first year of operation and $20,900,000 for the second year. The General Assembly of 1937[4] figured to increase salaries 10 per cent to operate the 8-months' school and to provide for free books. The January, 1939 General Assembly was confronted with the following: (1) increasing salaries; (2) expanding Vocational Education; (3) providing for a Twelfth grade; (4) providing for a retirement system; (5) providing for the

<hr>

[2] Biennial Report 1936-38; p. 52.

[3] Biennial Report 1938-40; pp. 98, 100, 102.

[4] *Ibid.*, p. 12.

exceptional child; and (6) strengthening the law with reference to tenure, compulsory attendance, and allowing districts to vote supplements. It took daring statesmanship to resolve such weighty problems in the midst of a depression and at a time when the world was on the brink of global war.

To meet these challenges, the Legislature of 1933 created the School Commission which replaced the old Equalization Board. The School Commission began in 1935-36. One of its first acts was to provide free text-books;[5] giving pupils a choice of buying or renting. At first, sales were large, but after the first two years, they diminished as students began to rent the texts. Later the elementary texts became entirely free, while high school texts remained on a rental basis, although Erwin had recommended free texts for both elementary and high school pupils.

In the implementing of these innovations, Negro pupils could share equally except, perhaps, in the case of Distributive Education, in which few could qualify, but under the George Dean Act, Negro pupils were generally found in the diversified occupations category. However, on the agenda of nearly every legislature of the Thirties, Negro Education was still a subject not wholly resolved. Legislatures of the late Thirties consistently made appropriations to lessen the salary differentials.

Erwin persistently reminded the Legislatures that because of a Court ruling in another State equalizing salaries, the State was under the necessity of bridging the gap between maximum and minimum salaries. "We have moved in that direction. If the Budget requirement of $250,000 to offset the differentials is approximated for each of the two years of this Biennium (1938-40) and for three or four additional years, the gap will be closed."[6]

In 1943 the General Assembly made the final appropriation ($507,500) for the elimination of salary differentials, which, beginning with the term, 1944-45 would equalize salaries paid by the State for white and Negro teachers. Any difference that remained would be found in local supplements paid to teachers.

Equality in teachers salaries was not the only item in the effort of the State to bridge the gap between the races in educational opportunities. Governor Melville Broughton recommended a study to be made of the Negro Public Schools and of the Colleges. Commenting upon the completion of the study, the State Superintendent said:

> That study is now completed and recommendations submitted to the State Board. It envisages a program covering a period of years for its final completion for improving public school facilities for the Negro. I heartily endorse any plans that may be projected. . . . The present provisions for edu-

---

[5] Biennial Report 1940-42; Publication No. 241, Part I; p. 74.

[6] Biennial Report 1938-40; p. 15.

cation for many Negro children are meagre to say the least. Better education for Negroes will not only raise the level of Negroes, but that of all the citizens of the State.[7]

Equality in length of terms between white and Negro schools is shown in a comparison of a period begining in 1919 and ending in 1945. In 1919-20 the length of the white school term in days was 135.9; of the Negro term, 127.4. By 1939-40, the status of the term for Negroes was just 2 percentage points less and by 1945 complete equality in length of school terms had been achieved with the figures for both races showing an average of 179.9 days.[8]

Equality in Training of Teachers

Strides toward Equality in educational opportunity were by no means limited to achieving equality in salaries and equal length of terms, but in the quality of training of the teachers. When it is recounted that as late as the early Twenties, the majority of Negro teachers had little more than an elementary education and that by the late Thirties most of them were holding college degrees, the progress toward equality assumes a remarkable status.

Equality in training had had its resurgence under Superintendent Brooks and his masterful lieutenants, A. T. Allen and N. C. Newbold in the early Twenties. During the early Thirties, this resurgence had no bounds. Negro teachers literally flooded the summer schools and many secured leaves of absence to study during regular terms. Hampton Institute offered the Master's degree in Education and many northern universities received Negro matriculates who earned graduate degrees.

White teachers reached their highest average in 1940-41 with an index of 793.3. Negro teachers attained their highest in 1944-45 with an index of 790.6.[9]

Approximately 90 per cent of the teachers and principals in 1948-50 held certificates based upon college graduation and above. The index of white teachers in 1940-41 was 793.3. By 1940-50 the Negro index had reached 804.2.[10]

Erwin was deeply conscious of the tremendous proportions of his job. "The State," he said, "Employing 25,000 teachers (1940) touching the lives of about a million children must be regarded as 'Big Business' ": and with the rapid rise in the training of teachers he thought it a remarkable progress. He said that the State was ready to project its program on the graduate level — making a Master's degree one requirement for administrative and supervisory positions

---

[7] Biennial Report 1942-44; Publication No. 251; p. 110.

[8] Biennial Report 1946-48; Publication No. 272; p. 16.

[9] Ibid., p. 16ff.

[10] Biennial Report 1948-50, Summary and Recommendations; p. 19.

and to recognize a graduate degree in certificiation of class-room teachers.[11]

Retirement Program

Realizing the fact that many of the State's older teachers who had borne the brunt of meagre salaries and short terms were gradually being displaced with little economic security, Erwin, in 1939, recommended to the General Assembly that a study of a retirement system be made and a report given to the Governor.[12]

Provisions to make such a study were made forthwith and the Retirement Act was inaugurated July 1, 1941. Of this very important innovation in educational circles in favor of so many teachers who faced retirement with hopeless anticipation, Erwin wrote:

> Teachers who now teach until they reach retirement age may face old age with assurance of some measure of security during their last days.[13]

Teacher Tenure

Because teachers were often victims of political and personal acts, Erwin thought that, next to a retirement program, a tenure law to protect teachers from insidious acts of local patronage would be an improvement in the selection of good teachers. He therefore, in 1938, recommended a tenure program to protect teachers from dismissal for political or petty reasons. Security, he said, would increase the instructional program and would make the welfare of children a first consideration.[14]

A modified continuing contract for teachers and principals from year to year was enacted by the General Assembly in 1941.[15]

The Twelve Year Program

The impetus of Brooks' and Allen's Administrations toward progressivism had motivated Erwin to forge North Carolina into the ranks of the most progressive states of the Nation. This motivation not only induced the public higher institutions to abandon secondary training, but inspired the private colleges to move into the ranks of accredited institutions. In addition, high schools and elementary schools were rapidly becoming standardized and accredited. One

---

[11] Biennial Report 1939-40; p. 39

[12] *Ibid.*, p. 112.

[13] Biennial Report 1940-42; p. 93.

[14] Biennial Report 1938-39; p. 117.

[15] Biennial Report 1942-44; Publication No. 251; p. 100.

entrance requirement of the colleges (both public and priavte) was
entrance requirement of the colleges (both public and private was
In the midst of the depression years, consideration had been
given to the establishment of an 8-4 grade plan. As early as 1921,
Roanoke Rapids had added a 12th grade on the 6-3-3 plan (six years
elementary; three years, junior high; and three years senior high).
New Hanover in 1923 had added the 12th grade. Charlotte in 1925-26
had organized a junior-senior plan with the senior high as the 10th,
11th, and 12th grades. A year later Durham added the 12th grade.
Hendersonville organized a 6-3-3 plan and Washington a 12th grade
in 1935-36. Rocky Mount followed in 1937.

Erwin noted that about 25 per cent of high school graduates
attended college of some kind and that an extra year of high school
at home would give an advantage to those desiring to go to college.
An appropriation of $50,000 was recommended to study a transition
to a 12th year system.[16]

The General Assembly of 1941 provided for the extension of
Public School System to embrace 12 grades; the cost, "to be paid for
the operation of the State's 8 months' school term." Bulletin 235, A
Suggested Twelve year Program, (with which all high school administrators were familiar) outlined the procedures of the 12 year
program. The curriculum was not radically changed; remaining 4
years of high school, build upon 8 years, instead of 7 years of elementary training.[17]

Accredited High Schools

Although many high schools for Negroes had been rated as
standard by the State Department even before the coming of the 12
Year program, only a few had been rated or had met the requirement
of the Association of Colleges and Secondary Schools, a rating agency
of high schools in the southern states.

From a letter dated December 17, 1934, from Fred McCuistion,
Executive Agent, Association of Colleges and Secondary Schools to
Superintendent Erwin, we have a list of the first Negro public high
schools to be accredited by the Southern Association:[18]*

Name of School	Location	Principal
Brick Tri-County High	Brick	T. S. Inborden
James B. Dudley	Greensboro	J. A. Tarpley
William Penn	High Point	S. E. Burford

---

[16] Biennial Report 1934-36; p. 12.

[17] Biennial Report 1940-42; p. 12.

[18] Letter, Fred McCuistion to Clyde A. Erwin, December 17, 1934; SPI Corr. File
Box 124.

* Dillard High in Goldsboro was accredited in 1937 — H. V. Brown, Principal.

Ridgeview	Hickory	A. W. Booker
Washington High School	Raleigh	M. W. Aikins
Washington High School	Reidsville	J. A. McRae
Williston	Wilmington	J. A. Carter

Vocational Education

In addition to vocational agriculture and vocational home economics for high schools, a course for farmers who were veterans of World War II was provided under a contract with the Veterans Administration which paid the tuition. Such courses would be set up wherever there was already a course in vocational agriculture. The State Board was responsible for the operation, supervision, and administration. The course could run from one to four years.

Occupational guidance was adopted in 1939 with Federal funds to strengthen the vocational education program and to assist the schools in developing better guidance activities.[19]

Resource Use Education

For the purpose of increasing emphasis in conservation and development of natural, social, and human resources in schools and community — how man draws on his environment — a commission was appointed in 1945 to establish a program to be known as "Resource Use Education."[20]

In 1943 the State took another long step in its enriched educational benefits in establishing the School Lunch Program. Although it entailed no curriculum assets, the School Lunch program posed objectively great lessons in dieting and in sanitation. Consultants at State level were appointed and in most consolidated and larger schools, lunch room workers became a part of the school systems.[21]

Prior to this point our story has dealt mainly with public education, but no story of education in our State could justly omit the excellent work and cooperation of the private higher institutions — denominational schools which existed throughout the period covered in this story. Without the beneficence of various philanthropic agencies and the help of the various religious and other private organizations, it would not have been possible to achieve the progress noted in the education of the Negro.

Even the progress in public education was greatly bolstered by private philanthropy which was not always available to the denominational schools. The record of most of the denominational schools is a story of tremendous struggles to keep alive in the face of financial difficulties. Many of them, perhaps, were created out of ambition

---

[19]Biennial Report 1946-48; Publ. No. 272; p. 38ff.

[20] Ibid., p. 69.

[21] Ibid., p. 50.

and jealousy of rival church leaders, who were often inspired by denominational zeal rather than by community need.

As late as 1915 when awareness of public responsibility toward secondary education was apparent, there were in the State 72 private (semi-boarding) institutions operated by Negroes. They reported an annual income of $262,032; property valued at over $2 million; enrollment of 7,828, of which 6,656 were elementary and 1,087 secondary. Of these 72 institutions, only 30 played any important part in the educational activities of the State. Some of the remaining 42 might have been justified upon denominational grounds.[22]

Based upon the extract from this report, (A Study of Private and Higher Schools for Colored People; Vol. II, U. S. Bureau of Education), N. C. Newbold induced most of the denominational schools to "sell out" to the State where the responsibility for secondary and elementary education belonged.[23]

The private colleges have all completely abolished preparatory or secondary courses and are all fully accredited four-year colleges. The public colleges, A&T College, Greensboro; Winston-Salem Teachers College in Winston-Salem; Fayetteville State Teachers College in Fayetteville; and Elizabeth City Teachers College in Elizabeth City are all four-year standard colleges; while North Carolina College at Durham not only is a four year liberal arts college, but has established a well-recognized graduate school.

North Carolina is indebted to the Baptists for Shaw University; to the Methodists for Livingstone College and Bennett College; to the Presbyterians for Johnson C. Smith University and Barber-Scotia College; to the Episcopalians for Saint Augustine's College, all of which for many years have been most helpful to the State in heightening the equality of education for its Negro citizens.

Clyde Erwin died in office July 19, 1952, after a tenure not equaled by that of any of his predecessors. His achievements as recounted by his successor, Dr. Charles F. Carroll, are a fitting climax to a life dedicated to the welfare of all the children of the State; and with this recount, we close the chapter on Clyde A. Erwin.

Erwin's Record

1. 1933   A State appropriation of $16 million plus $3¼ million from other sources for operation in 1934-35.

2. 1935-36   Completion of a rental system of text-books; made free to elementary pupils in 1937-38.

3. 1941   Enactment of a State Retirement System.

---

[22] Bulletin 1916, Bureau of Education, Washington, D. C., No. 39 — A Study of Private and Higher Schools for Colored People in United States; Vol. II; pp. 387ff.

[23] Brown, *Op. Cit.*, p. 66.

4. 1941   Establishment of a Twelfth Grade program.

5. 1941   Adoption of the Amendment to create a single "State
                Board of Education" to replace: the State Board of
                Vocational Educational Education, the ex-officio State
                Board of Education, The State Text-Book Commission,
                the State Board of Commercial Education, and the
                State School Commission.

6. 1943-44   Adoption of a uniform 9-Month's term.

7. 1943-44   Raising the Compulsory Attendance age from 14 to 16.

8. 1943-44   Equalization of white and Negro teachers' salaries.

9. 1943-44   Adoption of the School Lunch Program.

10. 1943-44   Creation of Special Education for the handicapped.

11. 1949   Adoption of a $50 million school plant construction
                and Improvement for expansion of school programs.

12. 1949   Passing of an amendment giving authority to allot
                supervisors and special teachers and Supervisor of
                Music at State level.

13. 1949   Appropriation of $550,000 to provide a State-wide
                health program.

14. 1949   Adoption of a Self-Insurance plan for school buildings
                and properties.

Chapter XI

The Administration of Charles F. Carroll
1952

Following the death of Clyde A. Erwin in 1952, Charles F. Carroll was appointed State Superintendent by Governor W. Kerr Scott and was elected to succeed himself in 1956 and in 1960. Born in Duplin County and educated at Trinity College (now Duke University), he successively held positions of educational leadership from teacher-coach of athletics, principal, and supervising-principal in various educational units in the State, and finally Superintendent of Schools in High Point before his appointment as State Superintendent of PublicInstruction.

Our story in this chapter will be concerned with the continued expansion of the educational services; some of the statistics of progress; curriculum additions; Negro leadership at state level; and finally the most revolutionary challenge to educational leadership, the Supreme Court Decision anent segregation in the public schools.

Throughout the story we have endeavored to show some physical progress in facts and figures which bear some light upon equality of opportunty as between white and Negro with particular inference to attendance at school; and at times, value of school property race-wise; length of term and comparative teachers' salaries until these last two items were wholly equalized. However, Equality in attendance, while not prohibitive, has not been wholly achieved either becauseof economic reasons or because of gross indifference among Negro parents and children.

Statistics

In the first report of Superintendent Carroll, which overlapped the final years of Clyde A. Erwin, enrollment figures are shown in Table I for 1950-52. Following, in Table II, the enrollment figures are given for 1950-62, a ten year period, the comparison of which should be carefully noted by students of such statistics. Of particular importance are the "Per cent" columns.

TABLE I — 1951-52

Race	Elem. Enr.	Av. Dai. Att.	%	High Sc. Enr.	Av. Dai. Att.	%
White	496,677	450,001	93.6	144,404	128,556	94.1
Negro	223,714	194,846	92.8	49,474	42,703	92.3[1]

[1] Biennial Report, 1950-52; p. 20.

133

Dr. Charles F. Carroll

State Superintendent of Public Instrucion

TABLE II — 1961-62

Race	Elem. Enr.	Av. Dai. Att.	%	High Sc. Enr.	Av. Dai. Att.	%
White	588,588	541,272	94.5	211,693	192,000	94.6
Negro	267,112	238,526	91.5	74,181	64,135	91.3[2]

It will be readily seen that enrollment figures for both races understandingly are higher over this ten year period, but while the per cent of attendance of white children increased, the per cent of attendance of Negro children actually decreased — a fact which cannot be ignored in the quest for "E-Qual-ity Education."

In the matter of "drop-outs," the score is more favorable to the Negro situation. For 1951-52, the per cent of white drop-outs was 5.0 while that of Negro drop-outs was 4.8;[3] for 1961-62 the score was, white 4.1 per cent; Negro 3.9 per cent.

Some further statistics which are more or less interesting and need to be studied concern progress of children. In 1962 approximately 96 per cent of the white enrollment and 90 per cent of Negro enrollment were promoted to the next higher grade. Thirty Six Thousand, Seven Hundred and Fifty Three white children, or 86.2 per cent were graduated in 1962. Of the 1961 graduates of white schools, 31.4 per cent entered a senior college; while 27.4 per cent of the Negro graduates of that year entered senior colleges.[4]

Taking these statistics as they are and for whatever reason they exist, it appears that Negro children do not have so good a record as white children in conscientiously accepting equal opportunity — a fact which should challenge all levels of Negro leadership.

Having been a teacher most of his life, the writer was keenly aware of the gross indifference of both parents and children with which they viewed the importance of a day lost out of school. Equality in Education has been sorely tried and frustrated by indifference.

Expansion of the State System

School legislation, year after year, had gradually brought control of education almost completely under the State Department of Public Instruction. Clyde Erwin had styled its dominance as "big business." Indeed it officially touched the lives of more people of the State than any other function of the State Government. Besides, no governmental department was better "stream-lined" for efficiency and progress.

Following is the organization as expanded in 1952-54: Aside from the State Superintendent, the Department of Public Instruction included: a general Assistant State Superintendent, an Administrative Assistant State Superintendent in Instruction (for the Divisions

---

[2] Biennial Report, 1960-62; p. 32 et seq.

[3] Biennial Report, 1952-54; p. 46.

[4] Biennial Report, 1960-62; pp. 35, 36.

of Elementary and Secondary Education, Negro Education, and School Health and Physical Education), a Coordinator of Teacher Education, and a professional staff in the following divisions:

1. Elementary and Secondary Education
2. Division of Negro Education
3. Division of Professional Services
4. Division of Publications
5. Division of Research
6. Division of School Planning
7. Division of Special Education
8. Division of School Health and Physical Education
9. Division of Vocational Education[5]

Because of the nature of the production, we are mentioning the names and positions of the Negro workers only. The Negro Division of Education as originally organized under N. C. Newbold as Director and later headed by G. H. Ferguson, no longer exists; Negro State workers being implemented into the various services with special attention to Negro schools.

In elementary education as supervisors are Frank B. Weaver and Mrs. Ruth L. Woodson; in Secondary Education: Frank A. Tolliver, Supervisor of High Schools and Harold H. Webb, Consultant in Special Education; in Guidance, Miss Thelma L. Cumbo, Consultant; in Library Service, Mrs. Doris L. Brown, Consultant; School Health and Physical Education, Mrs. Georgia Barbee, Health Coordinator; Home Economics, Mrs. Marie Moffitt, and Miss Augusta White, Assistant Supervisors: Vocational Trade and Industrial Education, James R. Taylor, Assistant Supervisor and Teacher Trainer; and Lunch Room Program, Mrs. Lois Brown and Mrs. Edna Trotter, Supervisors.[6]

Public schools are supported by Federal, State, and local funds. The amount of money expended for schools is staggering, but it demonstrates the confidence the public has developed for education. In 1953-54 the amount of Federal funds was $8 million, State funds, $119 million, and local funds $22 million.[7] Eight years later (1961-62) the amount expended was: Federal, $10,472,580; State $227,335,-129; and local, $47,493,150.[8]

---

[5] Biennial Report, 1952-54; p. 10.

[6] (Educational Directory 1962-63; p. 4 et seq.).
   (Corr. Ruth Woodson, Consultant Elementary Ed., State Department).

[7] Biennial Report, 1952-54; p. 20.

[8] Biennial Report, 1960-62; p. 98.

The value of school property has steadily mounted through the years. In 1896 the value of school property for white children was $654,925.75; for colored children, $223,206.60 or 26 per cent of the total values. In 1919-20 the value of school property for white children was $21,670,514; for colored children, $2,387,324 or 9.9 per cent of the total.[9] This was during the low period of interest in public acceptance of responsibility for Negro education. The interest began to resurge as we have seen under the administrations of Brooks and Allen and with the establishment of the Division of Negro Education under N. C. Newbold. By 1954-55 the percent of the value of school property for Negro children had risen to 20.6 per cent and by 1959-60 it reached 22.5 per cent.[10]

School building programs for Negroes were noticeably visible during the administration of Clyde Erwin, and have been greatly stepped up since the Supreme Court decision of 1954. Magnificent structures for Negro children are now found in almost every city and town and along paved rural highways in almost every county of the State. Some of those "architectural expressions" are illustrated in these pages.

Curriculum Expansion

In cooperation with Federal alertness to meet the ever developing needs of world competition, the State indorsed the program of the National Defense Act resulting in the establishment of industrial centers and certain courses for high school students which enable immediate entrance into economic living.

The National Defense Education Act was passed by Congress in 1958. Under this act funds were allotted to the States on a matching basis for the purpose of strengthening instruction in science, mathematics, and foreign languages. Some equipment acquisition and minor remodelling were permitted by the Act in 1961-62 the Federal Government matched in funds raised by local administrations the amount of $1,847,374.57.[11]

As early as 1959 studies were made in the State to determine the needs for programs of industrial education. A proposal for the development of a state-wide system of industrial education was adopted by the State Board of Education and subsequently by the General Assembly and the National Defense Act of 1958.[12]

Observation is made here, as was also made in Chapter IV, of the Administration of S. M. Finger, that industrial education had

---

[9] Biennial Report, 1952-54; p. 39.

[10] Biennial Report, 1958-60; p. 31.

[11] Biennial Report, 1960-62; pp. 84, 85.

[12] Brochure Trade and Industrial Education State Department of Public Instruction, p. 21.

been the "trade mark" of the Hampton philosophy and that of Booker T. Washington at Tuskegee as well as at some smaller institutions which had thrived upon the industrial philosophy. It had also been the feeling of many white educational leaders that the only necessary type of education for Negroes was industrial and agricultural.

With the development of automation, discoveries and innovations resulting from the war effort of 1917-18, most of the simple trades gradually became obsolete and the industrial programs of Hampton and Tuskegee were gradually or partially displaced by liberal arts and teacher training education. It appears that Negro educational leaders either lacked the means to secure necessary funds to develop new industrial or technical programs or failed to foresee the evolving industrial theory which was gradually seeping into the total economic life of the nation and thus lost the impetus which had been engendered by Hampton and Tuskegee.

When the industrial educational centers were started in North Carolina, Negroes were generally excluded, but the picture has been gradually, if not rapidly, changing as Negroes are now being accepted in many of the centers. Without their inclusion in this significant development, a large segment of Negro aspirants for industrial participation in the Nation's economic life would be permanently doomed.

The curricula of the industrial education centers are the best approaches to Quality Education for they are designed at the outset to make education function into actual life situations where economic need and the consequent remuneration are involved. Certainly the courses must be built upon the basic principles of mathematics and science, to say nothing about reading, writing, and English; but they are designed for entry into the many industrial and commercial pursuits by which the nation's economy exists.

These courses include training in almost every facet of living: electronics, with its various concomitants: communication, calculating systems, control systems, measuring and industrial systems; Industial Technicians; metal processing; tool design; various skilled trades; in short, courses for nearly every sort of function in the industrial economy of the present age.[13]

The Civil Rights report of 1960-61 showed that, among the nine industrial centers established at that time, there were 537 Negro students out of a total enrollment of 6,118 enrolled in the industrial education centers. They were enrolled in the following courses: electronics, mechanics, practical nursing, auto-mechanics, bricklaying, cosmetology, machine shop, air conditioning, cooking, tailoring, graphic arts and drafting. Two of these centers reported that they operated separate locations for Negroes and whites. One reported that the programs in the separate locations were different. Another center stated that segregation by race was followed in classrooms,

---

[13] *Ibid.*, pp. 23, 24.

lunchrooms, and restrooms. Six reported that there was no segregation in any of their facilities.[14]

Various and sundry reasons for the lack of Negro participation were reported by the Civil Rights Commission; not the least of these being the poor prospect of employment after completion of training. Poor prior training was also listed as a reason. Said one administrator:

> For admission an individual must present appropriate academic achievement in math, science, and English and related subjects as well as reasonable assurance he will profit from courses offered . . . courses offered in our industrial education center are technical and many can neither meet the requirement nor would they profit by taking the courses offered.

Another administrator stated that he had shown forty-seven Negroes through the school and invited them to apply for enrollment; that only four applied and that, of these, only one completed the necessary examination and he did so poorly that he could not be admitted. Still another administrator said that he had attempted to set up a program for Negroes, but that in many cases sufficient numbers had not applied or had not applied in time, or had failed to complete the examination.[15]

The situation with respect to the participation of Negroes in the industrial education centers doubtlessly has improved since the report of the Civil Rights commission of 1960-61 and will be included in the final chapter on Quality Education.

Distributive Education

One phase of the problem of admitting Negroes into certain courses stems from the philosophy that they are not generally engaged in certain types of employment. For example, Distributive Education, which provides training for those actually engaged in the distribution of goods and services, including training in fields of retailing, wholesaleing, banking, finance, transportation and like services, has generally been closed to Negroes. Certain high schools offer courses in Distributive Education to seniors, but the course has not been offered in Negro high schools.

However, as late as October, 1963, a bright ray of optimism appeared in a resolution of the Greensboro Merchants Association which requested the Greensboro Board of Education to make Distributive Education available to all senior high school students. Text of the resolution follows:

---

[14] Report of N. C. Advisory Commission — U. S. Commission on Civil Rights; pp, 92, 93.

[15] Ibid., pp. 96, 97.

We, the Merchants of Greensboro, are very earnest in our endeavor. We understand that difficulties of custom and privilege have separated much of our population in the past and we understand that this discrimination should and must be eliminated in the future. Consequently, the Greensboro Merchants Association requests the Greensboro City Schools to establish Distributive Education classes in all our senior high schools in order to assist our merchants in implementing this program. Better job opportunities are essential in the struggle against racial discrimination.[16]

In the high school program, the teacher-coordinator provides vocational guidance for the students interested in careers in some field of distribution, secures placement opportunities to provide work experience for student as trainees, gives instruction in the functions and practices of distribution and marketing, and develops an understanding of economic responsibilities and opportunities in the free enterprise system. Student-trainees also participate in the youth club program. Distributive Education Clubs of America, Inc. — which operates on local, state, and national levels to provide leadership development.[17]

As previously observed, a few Negroes, if any, have been included in the program of Distributive Education, but a corollary program, Trade and Industrial Education is being utilized for the training of many Negro students in a number of high schools. The program is financed from Federal, state, and local funds and includes (1) the high school and (2) an adult program.

The high school program includes students, sixteen years of age or older, who wish to learn a skilled trade or certain technical occupations. The latter is called "Diversified Occupations." In the former program, students spend three hours at trade classes and the remainder of the day in other high school subjects. In some high schools they work at "live projects" actually constructing dwellings.*

The Industrial Cooperative Training program (Diversified Occupations) is a cooperative program by the schools, business and industry to provide on-the-job training for youth in carefully selected occupational areas. This program is directed toward providing supervised occupational experience to enable student-learners to acquire skill and related technical information. In 1961-62 thirty-three high schools with an enrollment of 836 students were following the program. Students were receiving training in the following areas: auto-mechanics, building trades, cabinet making, dental assistance, and

---

[16]Editorial, *Greensboro Daily News,* October 7, 1963.

[17] Biennial Report, 1960-62; p. 66.

* Trade classes at Dillard High School, in Goldsboro, have constructed four dwellings and two additions to municipally owned buildings.

technicians, electrical trades, laboratory technicians, metal trades, nurses' aides, and in the printing trades.

The Adult Program offers pre-employment training and up-grading or up-dating of employed workers. Most of the adult program, however, falls into the realm of the industrial education centers, already described.[18]

Other educational programs which have sparked the Administration of Carroll include: Safety and Driver Education, Education of Exceptional Children, Exceptionally Talented Children, High School Equivalency, the Testing program, Audio-visual education, and Education by Television; all available upon a non-racial basis to all children. If there is any lack of participation in any of these programs on the part of Negro schools, it may conceivable be because of a lack of information thereof or indifference to innovations; perhaps sometimes local opposition.

Integration Race-Wise in the Public Schools

Perhaps the most revolutionary impact upon education in North Carolina (and in the entire South) since reconstruction was the United States Supreme Court decision of 1954 which declared that segregation in the public schools is unconstitutional.

Although not wholly unexpected, the decision aroused emotions varying from tacit acceptance in some states to massive resistance in others. The sentiment in North Carolina, though nowhere unanimous, was well expressed by State Superintendent Carroll:

> Any abrupt jolt to the customary pattern of thought and behavior of a large number of people, regardless of how noble the interest that propels, can produce grave repercussions; change, that is to endure, is born of consent on the part of a firm majority of the people who are to live with it ... the most notable observation is that no responsible North Carolinian has proposed the abolition of public education ... our basic prayer is that each of us will resolve anew that we shall preserve our cherished system of free public education in North Carolina.[19]

Though not germane to our story here, it must be said that some other states of the South assumed an entirely different view from that expressed by the leadership in North Carolina — either by actually closing some schools or by violently resisting efforts toward integration.

It is to the great credit of the State that Governor Luther Hodges took immediate steps to formulate a policy to resolve the great challenge without recourse to extremism. A committee headed by the Hon-

---

[18] *Ibid.*, p. 60, et seq.

[19] Biennial Report, 1952-54; p. 141.

orable Thomas J. Pearsall, a former State Legislator, was appointed to study the problem and to recommend a suitable plan whereby the State could live within the Court's decision.

On that committee were three Negro citizens: F. D. Bluford, President of A&T College, J. W. Seabrook, President of Fayetteville State Teachers College, and Mrs. Hazel Parker, Home Agent for Negroes in Edgecombe County.

When the sub-committee reported that: "The mixing of the races in the public schools cannot be accomplished and should not be attempted," President Seabrook threatened to submit a minority report. He finally induced the committee to insert the word, "forthwith"; for he held that the State could not permanently or indefinitely evade the Court's ruling. The word was inserted.[20]

Governor Hodges sought to secure tacit acceptance of the report among Negro leaders. He appealed to the "Leadership Conference" of the North Carolina Teachers Association (Negro) to adopt a policy of "voluntary segregation," but the Association declined to approve his proposal.

In addressing an assembly of students at A&T College, Greensboro the Governor was scarcely able to continue his address for the commotion among the students that created an embarrassing incident which President Bluford termed "reprehensible."

Apparently Negroes were not willing to decline a step which, obviously to them, was the greatest stride toward equality which had come to them since Lincoln's Emancipation Proclamation.

The 1955 session of the General Assembly enacted the Pupil Assignment Act with provisions by which local Boards of Education would assign pupils to the various schools under criteria to include the following:

1. The best interest of the child involved

2. Proper administration of the school

3. Proper instruction of the pupils therein enrolled

4. The health and safety of the children in schools

The Statute made no mention of race as a criterion for assignment and was adjudged constitutional on its face. However, various court cases designed to secure admission to all-white schools arose in different parts of the State. Most of them at first went against Negroes — the courts adroitly finding technicalities by which a case could be denied.

By 1957, the Greensboro, Winston-Salem, and Charlotte Boards of Education, with no suits pending against them, began assigning Negro students to previously all-white schools. In Wayne County, at Havelock, and other locations involving United State military bases

---

[20] Corr. J. W. Seabrook, Member of Pearsall Committee; January 7, 1963.

where children of military personnel attend, Negro children have been integrated into the schools since 1959.

The Meadow Lane School, located near Goldsboro, had 14 Negro children in 1949 and 17 in 1960. At Havelock in 1959 there were 17 and in 1960, 25 Negro children. Of the 334,200 Negro Students in the State in 1960-61, 226 or less than one-tenth of one per cent were enrolled in integrated schools: Including those students who were attending schools serving military bases. However, several administrative units in 1961-62, announced additional assignments for the 1962-63 term. Some of these were Brevard, Clinton, Fayetteville, Goldsboro, Salisbury, and Wilmington.

In 1961, the following administrative units made the following transfers to previously all-white schools: Asheville 5, Charlotte-Mecklenburg 27, Durham 4, Greensboro 8, Harnett 20 (all Indians), High Point 6, Raleigh 9, Winston-Salem 6, and Yancey County 3.

A tabulation of desegregated schools up to and including 1961 follows:

Communities	Years Desegregated	No. Non-Whites
Asheville, Newton Center	1961	5
Chapel Hill		
Carboro Elementary	1961	4
Estes Hill Elementary	1960	6
Glenwood Elementary	1961	20
Chapel Hill Junior High	1961	4
Charlotte-Mecklenburg		
Bethune Elementary	1960	15
Derita Elementary	1961	3
Dilworth Elementary	1961	5
Wesley Heights Elementary	1961	3
Harding High	1957	0 (1)
Garinger High	1957	0 (2)
Myers Park High	1961	1
Durham		
Fuller Elementary	1961	1
Brogden Junior High		
Carr Junior High	1959	14
Durham High		
Greensboro		
Gillespie Park Elem. and Jun. High	1957	15
Greensboro Senior High	1957	0 (2)
Harnett County		
Dunn High	1961	20 (3)
Havelock (Craven County)		
West Havelock Elementary	1959	14
Graham Barden Elementary	1959	19
Havelock Junior High	1961	2

High Point
Montlieu Elementary	1961	2
Ferndale Junior High	1959	5

Raleigh
Murphy Elementary	1960	2
Daniels Junior High	1961	5
Needham Broughton High	1961	3

Wayne County
Meadow Lane	1959	25

Winston-Salem
Easton Elementary	1958	13
R. J. Reynolds High (Adv. Plc't Crs)	1959	7

Yancey County
East Yancey High	1960	5
Cane River High	1960	4 (21)

1. Student withdrawn

2. Student graduated

3. All Indian Students

Later reports on integration in the State (1963) were not available when the preceding transcript was secured, but the figures are known to be increasing as more units each year are reported in the press as transferring some Negro children to previously all-white schools.*

Although the policy and practices in desegregation of public schools has been only token, it has provided no serious incidents. Negro students have made satisfactory progress and some have been graduated from these integrated schools. In several of the colleges, Negroes have been accepted and at the University of North Carolina, a Negro, Junius L. Chambers, was chosen as Editor-in-Chief of the *University Law Review*. Chambers was given a fellowship to Columbia University to study for the doctor's degree in the field of law.

The experiment, as implied in the Pearsall Committee report, apparently has disproved the committee's conclusion that "Mixing of the races in the public schools cannot be accomplished forthwith and should not be attempted."

Any attempt to give a full appraisal of the effect of integration upon public education at this time could hardly be just or fair in consideration of the small numbers involved and the brief period of trial, but there is one result of unmistakable appraisal in the erection of school buildings for Negro children. As mentioned before magnificent "architectural expressions" in Negro school buildings are being

---

* Goldsboro High School enrolled one Negro student in 1962, two additional ones in 1963, five to the Junior High, and one to Grammar School — all previously all-white schools.

erected in every part of the State. In addition, to help meet the challenge of Quality Education, these buildings are being adequately equipped with the best of educational facilities. How Negro students will accept or meet the challenge may well be the subject of public interest as well as their own alertness to justify the monumental strides toward Equality of Opportunity which have been made during this age.

The story of the Administration of Charles F. Carroll cannot be closed here for the reason that his administration has not ended. Charles F. Carroll was still the State Superintendent at the time this book was being written. However, the story recounts some of the significant recommendations of Carroll which point to progress in prospect for 1963-65; and with these recommendations, the chapter fittingly closes an era of progress and prospect of a great public servant.

First, let us see some comparisons of facts and figures over a 10 (and 11) year period from 1950-51 to 1960-61 (some facts of 1961-62).

The population of the State in 1950 was 3,014,576 white and 1,047,353 Negro people or a total of 4,061,929. Ten years later, 1960, the population was 3,440,134 white and 1,116,021 Negro or a total of 4,556,155. School enrollment for 1950-51 was 636,505 white; 273,272 Negro. Ten years later, 1960-61, it was 789,629 white; 334,200 Negro. First Grade enrollment in 1950-51 was 70,317 white; 39,666 Negro. Ten years later, 1960-61, it was 77,752 white; 39,406 Negro, a decrease of 2.2 per cent in Negro enrollment in the first grade. In the seventh grade in 1950-51, the enrollment was 55,227 white; 21,891 Negro. Ten years later, 1960-61, it was 74,929 white; 29,700 Negro.

Graduates in 1950-51 were 24,288 whites, 6,524 Negro, Ten years later, 1960-61, the number of graduates were 74,929 white; 29,700 Negro. The percentage of whites continuing their education in 1950-51 was 44.6 per cent; Negro 41.2 per cent. Ten years later, 1960-61, 54.4 per cent of the white graduates and 39 per cent of Negro graduates continued their education: the Negro record being decreased .2 per cent.

In transportation 317,972 white children and 92,720 Negro children were transported in 1950-51. Ten years later the figures were 393,922 whites and 156,249 Negro.

In the appraised value of school property, the period covers eleven years, from 1950-51 to 1961-62 and exhibits a remarkable increase in the per cent of evaluation of Negro school property over that of white school property. In 1950-51 the value of white school property was $235,852,975; that of Negro school property was $46,705,140. In 1961-62 (11 years) the value of white school property was $647,905,892, an increase over 1950-51 of 174.7 per cent while the value of Negro school property was $181,779,608 or an increase of 289.28 per cent. Applying this evaluation over a per pupil basis, in 1950-51, it was 370.54 per white pupil; $170.91 per Negro pupil;

while in 1961-62, it was $809.60, or 118.5 per cent per white pupil; and $537.62 or 211.6 per cent per Negro pupil.

This story does not begin to pretend that educational facilities in the State are entirely equal, but it is apparent that great strides have been made to accord equal opportunity for every child to burgeon out the best there is in him. The State is obligated to give every child an equal chance to develop into the best possible citizen; conversely, the child is obligated to employ his talents to the highest extent in order to make the best contribution of which he might be capable.

Let us now observe some of the comments and recommendations of Superintendent Carroll in his biennial report of 1960-62:

> North Carolina has not yet achieved its educational potential. There are still too many children out of school. There are still too many small schools with a restricted curriculum. There are still too many children leaving school before graduating. There are still too many high school graduates who cannot or do not continue their education. There are still too many teachers with too many children in their classes. There are still too many superintendents and principals with too little time to devote to educational planning and instructional improvements. There are still too few librarians and counselors and supervisory personnel. There are still too many children and too many schools without adequate books, instructional supplies, and classroom equipment. These inadequacies are the opportunities which have been translated into a "B" Budget.

Because this budget is of great importance to administrators and teachers, and is a projection into the immediate future, it is recorded here in full.

"B" Budget for 1963-65

I Secure and hold better qualified teachers and principals

    A. Raise teachers salaries by $15 per month the 1st year and an additional $10 per month the 2nd year of biennium . . . to make North Carolina salaries competitive with the National average. (N. C. avr. 1961-62 $4877; National $5527) $ 15,420,097.00

    B. Provide up to 5 days sick leave per year for teachers and cumulative as now provided for other state employees   2,623,260.00

    C. Adjust and provide approximately 4% increase in principals' salaries and adjust the length of term by size and type of school   1,787,288.00

D. Provide additional scholarships for students preparing to teach (150 the first year and and an additional 150 the second year)   157,500.00

Total $ 19,988,145.00

II Provide improved classroom teaching conditions so that students will have better chance to learn

A. Allot teachers each spring on the basis of students who will be in school the following year rather than enrollment the current year $ 4,769.376.00

B. Change allotment formula of additional teachers to reduce class size, provide librarians, guidance counselors, special education teachers, teachers of the gifted, and teachers to relieve principals of teaching duties from 1 to 20 to 1 to 15 regular allotted teachers   5,360,567.00

C. Change the fall allotment for rapidly growing schools from 32 to 31 pupils in Avr. dail. att.   2,466,302.00

D. Provide additional vocation teachers in the IEC; and provide additional home economics, trade and industrial, and distributive educational teachers in H. S.   3,784,396.00

E. Provide additional special allotment teachers for mentally retarded students (100 the first year and an additional 100 for the second year)   1,407,042.00

F. Provide additional special allotment teachers for exceptionally talented students (158 the first year an additional 15 the second year)   1,555,362.00

G. Provide teachers for children who are kept in the hospital because of illness or handicaps   100,000.00

H. Increase state appropriation for trainable, mentally handicapped children   145,782.00

I. Provide 150 attendance counselors to help the absence and drop-out problem   1,409,428.00

Total $ 20,998,255.00

III Provide professional help for teachers

A. Provide 60 additional supervisors   791,667.00

B. Provide the same salary increase for supervisors as for teachers ($15 and $25)   141,200.00

C. Extend the in-service education program for teachers to training in the teaching of reading on which all academic instruction depends   200,000.00

     Total $ 1,132,867.00

IV   Give Teachers and Students the tools they need

A. Provide a subsidy of $4.00 per high school student in order to get up-to-date textbooks into hands of students without adding to fees charged   2,439.244.00

B. Provide funds to buy films to be used in instruction (25c per pupil in A.D.A)   571,590.00

C. Provide for equipment needed for new I.E.C.   2,000,000.00

     Total $ 5,010,834.00

V   Improve special service for the handicapped
A. Increase state aid for the vocational rehabilitation, $150,000.00 of which is to make up for free college tuition not now provided   324,783.00

VI   Improve local educational leadership

A. Provide 48 assistant superintendents in larger school units   855,360.00

B. Increase school clerical salaries by 5%   80,750.00

     Total   936,110.00

VII   Improve State Educational leadership under State Board of Education

A. Improve fiscal service in Controller's office $ 240,937.00

B. Improve State service in Vocational Education   345,047.00

C. Improve administration of Vocational Rehabilitation   19,072.00

D. Expand State level school planning service in education by television   43,912.00

E. Expand State level service to local units in school planning   109,272.00

F.	Extend State service in administering the National Defense Education program	73,959.00
G.	Expand State service in the exceptionally talented child programs	116,124.00
	Total	$ 948,323.00

VIII Increase State financial help to local school units in school plant operation and transportation

A.	Provide 173 additional janitors and maids	$ 294,222.00
B.	Increase funds for operation of plants	1,186,200.00
C.	Increase bus drivers' salaries by $2.50 per month to make this $30 per month	409,732.00
	Total	$ 1,890,250.00
	Grand Total	$ 51,229,567.00

Carroll's final recommendations for improving publc education in the State follow:

1. To consolidate schools and to merge school-administrative units

2. To construct school facilities of such type and design as will best accommodate comprehensive education programs

3. To expand and extend school transportation service for children attending both rural and urban schools

4. To protect investments in school facilities by increasing personnel and funds for maintenance and operation

5. To broaden the scope of educational opportunities in North Carolina by providing:

   a. Summer school education

   b. Kindergarten education

   c. Adult education

6. To study and strengthen the scope, sequence, and content of vocational education at both high school and post high school levels, with particular emphasis on the program in the senior high school

7. To study teacher education as it relates to the cultivation of the competence needed in our contemporary culture

8. To study teacher performance and devise some acceptable methods for identifying and rewarding superior service

9. To strengthen State-level services to local schools through the employment of additional consultants in the State Department of Public Instruction

10. To strengthen the qualifications for membership on boards of education and school committees.

11. To strengthen instruction at all levels by

    a. Identifying and recognizing the varying abilities of children through testing guidance

    b. Planning curriculum compatible with varying potentialities of youth and by establishing programs that challenge those potentialities

    c. Organize the school curriculum and schedule in such manner as to record priority to the teaching process

    d. Increasing expenditures for basal and supplementary text-books, for library books, and instructional materials and equipment

    e. Experimenting with newer methods and media of instruction

    f. Intensifying in-service education of all — personnel — teachers, administrators, supervisors, and service personnel

    g. Evaluating the school and seeking accreditation by the State and by the Southern Association of Schools and Colleges

12. To study and appraise plans for financing public education with particular consideration being given to those patterns of finance which involve State, federal, and local governmental agencies in a joint relationship, with each of the three levels of government assuming a proportionate share of the cost based on need, effort, ability, and performance[22]

Such were the dreams — the foresight of the man whom Governor W. Kerr Scott appointed in 1952 and the people elected in 1956 and in 1960 to guide North Carolina toward a more respectable position with the states of the Nation.*

---

[22] Biennial Report, 1960-62; p. 97 et seq.

* The following among Carroll's recommendations were activated in 1963. *Goldsboro News Argus,* October 25, 1963, p. 1.

1. Teachers granted 5 day cumulative sick leave a year.

2. More teachers for mentally retarded, physically disabled and otherwise handicapped; 200 such over 2-year period.

3. Hiring 150 more special teachers for gifted children.

4. $1½ million for experimental program in trade and industrial education.

5. Add money for increasing I.E.C. over State.

6. School bus drivers salary $30 per month.

7. Salary of teachers and superintendents increase $15 per month 1st year and $10 2nd year of biennium.

8. $10 per month salary increase for mechanics and clerks

9. Allotments to school administration units increased by 5% for clerical workers in Superintendent's office.

10. Compulsory attendance law strengthened with provision of 61 attendance counselors.

11. Expansion in prospective teacherse scholarship loan program.

12. Power to use appro. bala. to cut out bank rental fee.

---

[23] *Goldsboro News-Argus,* October 25, 1963, p. 1.

Dillard High School, named for the Reverend C. Dillard, was built in 1957 and dedicated under the principalship of the author.

Its present principal is John H. Wooten, a pupil of the author.

Bynum Elementary School — Kinston

Norwayne School — Wayne County

Chapter XII
Quality Education

As we enter upon the final chapter of "E-Qual-ity Education," we remind the reader that, without doubt, he has observed that the previous chapters have borne the title, "Administration of . . ."; and that frequent reference has been made to the title of the story as: "E-Qual-ity Education." Now that these previous chapters have exhausted the effort to explore the strides toward "Equal Opportunity," it remains for the final chapter to describe the other inference of the subject, "Quality" in the current emphasis upon Education among Negroes in North Carolina.

As inferred, if not actually asserted in the preface, the psuedonym, E-Qual-ity, would allude to the terms equal and also to quality.

In the previous chapters the story has endeavored in a factual manner to illustrate the development of opportunity toward which the State's public educational system has moved throughout the administrations of the various State Superintendents from Calvin Wiley in 1867 to Charles F. Carroll in 1963.

The story does not — cannot — claim that a state of absolute equality, or even equality of opportunity has been fully achieved, but no one possessed with genuine objectivity can read these chapters without recognizing enormous strides in the direction of complete equality of opportunity.

This chapter, Quality Education, must necessarily be one more of philosophy than of history, for it will endeavor to demonstrate the ideas and philosophies of current advocates of educational doctrine. What educational leaders, white and Negro, are doing at State level; what critics say and propose for educational improvement; what influence integration is having upon progress; the Governor's "assault on poverty" program; the impact of Negro demonstrations for freedom; the prospect of greater participation in industrialization; and some examples of the emphasis of Quality Education as pursued in the schools will, in the main, form the content in this closing chapter.

In the introduction to the story there were included several definitions or descriptive ideas of what is meant by "Quality Education." Included among those from former co-workers of the author was that of the State Superintendent. Of course, none of these are identical. In fact there can be no single explanation or description of Quality Education, but all added up to the summation of doing one's best with what he has at his command.

Where did the term, "Quality Education," originate? Perhaps that is not known, but it is fairly certain that the emphasis in North Carolina had its genesis with Governor Terry Sanford who wrote the author:

I believe the term, Quality Education, was first used in an address I made to women of the Greensboro area during the first primary in 1960. Of course, our point in talking about Quality Education was that North Carolina needed not only universal education, but needed also the highest quality of education possible.[1]

The term quickly became an educational slogan just as Aycock's *"Universal Education"* became a battle cry early in the century. Quality Education is not a method in the sense that "Progressive Education," the Project Method, the Platoon System of Teaching, and many other experimental programs were methods, but Quality Education is a new emphasis which doubtlessly Education needed to inspire a more vigorous interest in these days of international competition. It is certainly a good emphasis — easily comprehended and easily explained even to the youngest of school children. It is also an enduring emphasis for the time will not come when quality in education will not be desired. Nor has there ever been a time when there was not quality. Picture the philosophy of some early educational "barb" who wrote so applicably:

> Good, better, best,
> Never let it rest
> 'Till your good is better
> And your better, best.

Whoever wrote these simple lines perhaps had never thought of the term, Quality Education, but his motivation compares favorably with the philosophy of current educators.

Educational systems, or practices, have always had critics among laymen as well as among educators themselves; and what they say should not always be disregarded. There might be a measure of sincerity enough for Educators to regard as challenges for evaluation of programs and practices rather than as mere criticism to ignore.

A good example of criticism is that of Vice-Admiral H. G. Rickover, a layman. (From a copywrited Associated Press Story, March 17, 1963).

Vice Admiral Rickover is one of the most out-spoken men of the times and states what he thinks is wrong and what he thinks should be done about it. Says the Vice-Admiral:

> American education just isn't good enough . . . the best is to stretch their minds and reach the highest goals their intellect can encompass.

He states that our schools are markedly inferior to the schools of the countries with which we are competing economically and politically; that:

---

[1] Letter to H. V. Brown from Governor Terry Sanford, October 17, 1963.

We can no longer affort to waste money on an inadequate school system. We have the shortest day and the shortest school year among leading nations. . . We should eliminate from the curriculum everything that can be learned elsewhere. We are the only advanced country where precious hours are wasted teaching children how to make fudge, twirl batons, drive cars, budget income, handle the telephone, catch fish, and similar trivia that any reasonably normal person picks up on his own at home.

Rickover advocates a "National Scholastic Standing"; a national standing committee to formulate criteria which would in no way interfere with established institutions in granting degrees or diplomas. The committee would provide a set of examinations at appropriate levels of students who might wish to prepare for semi-professional or technical positions not requiring a bachelor's degree, but still requiring a good high school education. The notation, "N.S." (National Scholar) would be stamped upon the degree of those who pass the examination.[2]

What effect Vice Admiral Rickover's suggestion has had upon current educators is not known by this author, but it is certain that he has thrown out a great challenge to all who would have American education compete with that in other countries.

Another lay-man, Malcomb Seawell, North Carolina Attorney-General in 1959, while not specifically criticising education, prophetically alerts educators (and tax-payers, as well) to the need for good education, in the prospect of the bulging population and industrialization between now and 1975. Says Mr. Seawell:

North Carolina is estimated to get a population increase of 1,750,000 by 1975. This expansion will require housing, clothing, food, transportation, and education. To meet this growth in population and the constantly expanding industrial development, North Carolina must have good schools.[3]

Dr. Conant (James B. Conant, no layman nor novice in the field of Education) has written a notable work, *The Education of American Teachers,* Copyright, 1963, in which he bases his criticism of education upon the training of teachers. He holds that there is little unanimity among the colleges of teacher education either in curricula or in evaluation of credits; and that administrations are generally not consistent in placing teachers entirely in the fields in which they have been trained.

In the concluding paragraph of his observations, Dr. Conant states:

---

[2] *Greensboro Daily News,* March 17, 1963; Sec. A., p. 8.

[3] *Ibid.,* February 1, 1959; Sec. D., p. 5.

In any discussion about the idea of a liberally educated man, one encounters differences of opinion as to what this expression means; and there is a great variety of programs reflecting these diverse opinions.

We list here some of his observations which might be of interest, if not of real value, to public school officials who do not fear to listen to criticism. To all persons interested in education, from the tax-payer who looks at his tax dollar to the educator who looks beyond to his country's security, we recommend Dr. Conant's book as a profoundly objective approach to the knotty problem of training of teachers. Note the following from Conant's *"The Education of American Teachers"*:

1. The State education authorities should give top priority to the development of regulations insuring that a teacher will be assigned only to those teaching duties for which he is specifically prepared, and should enforce these regulations rigorously.

2. The State should provide financial assistance to local boards to insure high-quality practice teaching as part of the preparation of teachers enrolled in either private or public institutions.

3. School boards or the State should provide financial assistance so that teachers may attend summer school after enrolling in a graduate school for the purpose of completing a program for salary increment.

4. School board should provide leave of absence with salary for a full-time residence at a university to enable teachers to study toward a master's program, providing this program is designed to increase competence of the teacher; State funds should be available for this purpose.

5. All future elementary teachers should engage in practice teaching for a period of at least 8 weeks, spending a minimum of 3 hours a day in the classroom; the period must include at least 3 weeks full responsibility for the classroom under direction of a cooperating teacher and the supervision of a clinical professor.[4]

Many other critics of educational standards, with particular reference to its impact upon Negro aspirations for equality, are doubtlessly just as sincere as they are critical. With benefit of any doubt, their criticism is hardly designed to provoke anger or even controversy, but to inspire greater effort toward attaining quality in education and consequently equality of opportunity.

---

[4] Conant, James B., *The Education of American Teachers*, pp. 209, et seq.

Dr. William C. Archie, Director of the State Board of Higher Education for North Carolina, speaking before the convention of the North Central District, N. C. Teachers Association, at Selma, N. C. on November 6, 1963, observed that disadvantaged children do so poorly in school because they come from disadvantaged homes — homes which often have not even a newspaper or any other literature except the Bible; that many teachers today have come from such homes. "Separate, but equal," he said, "is a fallacy which has produced much of the disadvantaged status of Negro children," continuing he said:

There are a great many things wrong . . . we have made progress, but not enough . . . the situation cannot be changed over night. Negro pupils must become qualified and to do so, the level of expectation must be raised. If a pupil can make an "A", we must expect an "A"; for opportunity means responsibility.[5]

Prominent leaders among Negroes, both educators and laymen, realize the inadequacies of Negro education and, while not actually critical of educational content or practices, apparently seek to motivate the Negro student's attitude by inspiring him to make the best use of his talents within the frame work of existing circumstances by exercising his full potential. It should not be assumed that these critics among Negro leadership are satisfied with the limited opportunities afforded by poor educational facilities or by inferior teaching, but obviously are implying that Negro pupils are not doing as well as they can with the opportunities at hand.

Dr. Samuel W. Byuarm, Professor of Sociology at Johnson C. Smith University, Charlotte, North Carolina, and his co-professor, Mack Davidson who teaches economics make the point that the Negro must qualify as he moves into what Dr. Byuarm calls, "The new social order." Said Dr. Byuarm:

The Negro from this point forward will have to prepare himself to compete with the whole society . . . the initiative is his . . . he will have to measure up. Whatever accomplishments the Negro will make are apt to be futile if not sustained by an excellence of preparation and performance.

Professor Davidson advocates an accelerated training program for Negroes to prepare themselves better to step into better jobs and to off-set handicaps of the past. Dr. Byuarm says further:

The Negro parent faces a tremendous responsibility of trying to decide whether he should train his child for a job he might get rather than for one he knows he will not get . . .

---

[5] Address, Dr. William C. Archie, Director, State Board For Higher Education; N. C. Teacher Dist. Teachers Convention, Selma, N. C., November 1, 1963.

Training is the key to the Negro's future in the new social order.[6]

Dr. Rudolph Jones, President of Fayetteville State College, relative to Negro recent demonstrations for equality, had the following to say:

If they would show as much militancy with their textbooks as they do in their demonstrations, we would be able to lick this segregation problem.[7]

Prior to the above, President Jones is alleged to have made a statement which was widely criticized, yet must have triggered an introspection among his teachers and graduates to ascertain if they might be victims of his assertion. What President Jones is alleged to have said is:

We admit illiterates, keep them four years, and when we graduate them, they are still illiterate.

This was a profound admission, but President Jones was hardly fair to himself, his institution or to those schools from which his students came, but the statement strikes at a vital point — lack of adequate preparation before and after — a vicious cycle in education which challenges all advocates of Quality Education.

Louis E. Lomax, a noted Negro writer, quite bluntly admonishes:

The generation of young Negroes that is doing so much to win new opportunities for itself is ill-equipped to use these opportunities. With splendid courage, these youngsters are breaking down barriers of prejudice. Yet they are not qualified for new jobs in industry and government now open to them. Even worse, Negro students often fail to show even a desire to get ahead.[8]

In September, 1963, New York State had to abandon a sincere effort to employ graduates of Southern Negro colleges because too few could pass the basic qualifying examinations.

One possible remedy, in a consensus of North Carolina Negro educators, would be a crash program to overcome academic deficiencies in a segregated society and foster by inadequate Negro graded and high schools. The first step, President Jones (Dr. Rudolph Jones, Mentioned above) suggests:

To gain a realization on the part of the teachers that these students are weak. They have been sweeping the dirt under

---

[6] *Greensboro Daily News*, June 16, 1963.

[7] *Ibid.*, October 13, 1963; p. A-9.

[8] *Ibid.*

DR. RUDOLPH JONES
President, State College,
Fayetteville

the rug for too long. If you pretend your students are better than they are, your case is hopeless.

Taking a cue from Author Lomax's suggestion that Negro "demonstrators" stage "study-ins" for "sit-ins," *The Goldsboro News-Argus* suggested that such a movement be tried for local consideration. Accepting the challenge, the Youth Council of the National Association for the Advancement of Colored People began a "study-in" school in October, 1963 with Mrs. H. F. Cofield, Director.[9]

Efforts Within the State

Critics in North Carolina — educators, laymen, and taxpayers — should recognize the fact that the State, including its educationally minded Governor, is making a serious effort to effect a genuine attitude for Quality Education among students as well as among teachers and parents, however, imperceptible it may appear to some. The recognition of equality of opportunity and of Quality Education of all children has become conscionable among educational and lay leaders who are translating that recognition into positive activity.

Some of this activity is evidenced through additions of qualified Negro leadership to the State Department of Public Instruction, through improved school facilities for Negro pupils, through integration of Negroes into previously all-white schools, by means of the expansion of industrial education programs, the Governor's School for Gifted High School Students, and his more recent "Assault on Poverty" program. In addition to these topics, there will appear in this final chapter some aspects of the "social revolution" reflected in the large scale unrest among Negro youth and its impact upon the State's conscience.

Finally, the story will specify some samples of effort among institutions to motivate students to develop the highest achievement of which they are capable.

Positive evidence that the State is endeavoring to provide good schools and adequate equipment for Negro children is illustrated in the many fine school buildings being erected in various parts of the State. However, as expressed by State Superintendent Charles F. Carroll at the dedication of the new Adkin Senior High School of Kinston, November 3, 1963, "A good school building does not make a good school"; buildings and equipment cannot guarantee "Quality Education," . . . a good school building merely provides the setting for a good school."[10]

Yet it is to the eternal credit of State and Local pride and initiative that these magnificent structures are being erected.

---

[9] *Goldsboro News-Argus,,* October 7, 1963; Editorial.

[10] Address, Charles F. Carroll; Dedication, Adkin High School, November 3, 1963.

Adkin High School — Kinston, North Carolina

Darden High School — Wilson, North Carolina

Pictures of some of these stuctures are exhibited but, while the story behind the erection of all of them is a notable expression of the increasing sentiment of taxpayers, that description is limited to a single sample herein described: Adkin Senior High School, Kinston; erected, 1963.

The site of the Kinston school, approximately 15 acres, was purchased for $51,784.57. It rises to magnificent heights overlooking the city with the potential for the finest landscaping in the city.* The estimated cost of the proposed structure (1960) was $800,000.00, including the site. The building contains 30 classrooms, including three science and biology rooms, chemistry and physics laboratory; separate commercial, typing, and bookkeeping rooms with office and work room space; two home economics rooms; physical education room, complete with showers, dressing rooms, and lockers; hygiene classroom, library, cafeteria to seat 300 students, with fully equipped kitchen and related services. The auditorium is equipped with upholstered seats for 760. The administrative section includes the Principal's office, secretaries' office, and waiting room; two guidance rooms, health room and teachers' lounge.[11]

This description of a new school for Negro pupils can be duplicated in many cities and in rural districts. Adkin Senior High is but a sample of the pattern which has been developing over the State in recent years.

Just how well Quality Education will vie with this magnificent structure depends upon the leadership of its fine Principal, C. B. Stewart, the cooperation of his faculty, the support of his parents, and the attitude of his students — all working together to achieve the highest possible results of which all (principal, teachers, parents, and children) are capable. (None of these can be omitted, for Quality Education is a "chain reaction" and no link can be left out).

E. E. Miller, principal of one of the leading high schools in the east has a well organized program geared to high quality training.

The State Department, including the Office of the Governor, Terry Sanford, has endeavored to move ahead in its recognition of Quality Education by adding to its staff competent and experienced Negro consultants or supervisors to help promote Quality Education and improve employment conditions among Negroes. It will be recalled that during the existence of the Division of Negro Education, there were only two Negro workers at State level in the Department of Education; there had been a consultant with the State Board of Health and a consultant with the State Board of Welfare. Currently (1963) seventeen Negro workers, including two appointees by the Governor, are working at State level.

---

* Formerly, planners for Negro schools took little thought of the site, except too often buildings were placed out of sight. That, too, has changed.

[11] Dedication Program — Adkin High School, November 3, 1963.

E. E. Smith High School — Fayetteville, North Carolina

164

E. E. MILLER
Principal, E. E. Smith High School,
Fayetteville

Mrs. Georgia W. Barbee is a consultant with the School Health Coordinating Service to supervise and consult with teachers in promoting standardized health practices among pupils throughout the schools of the State.

Mrs. Doris L. Brown, who for fifteen years was school librarian at Dillard High School in Goldsboro, assists the State Librarian and consults with school librarians in raising the standard of usefulness of school libraries.

Mrs. Lois Brown is a supervisor of the State School Lunch Service. Speaking of the impact of the service upon Quality Education, Mrs. Brown states:

An effective educational program depends upon mentally and physically alert youngsters. A hot, nutritious lunch plays an important role in helping a child understand and retain subject matter.

Miss Thelma L. Cumbo is a consultant in the all-important program of Guidance, so much needed in these days of frustration and aspirations of high school pupils.

Mrs. Sarah J. Herbin was appointed in 1963 by Governor Sanford as a consultant in Employment Services. Her function is to seek to discover qualified Negro aspirants or applicants for employment wherever employment is available.

W. T. Johnson is the Western District Supervisor of Vocational Agriculture. He is also Executive Secretary of the New Farmers Association, a club organization of the Smith-Hughes Vocational Agriculture program.

John R. Larkin has been the consultant for Negro welfare work since 1942. His interests range over the whole spectrum of Negro life. His unpublicized and official activities include helping Negro students get into college and advising them and seeking scholarships. Although attached to the Welfare Department, he works with and through numerous state departments.

Mrs. Marie Moffitt is one of the assistant Home Economics supervisors whose function is to work with Home Economics teachers in the high schools.

James R. Taylor, Assistant Supervisor and Teacher Trainer of Vocational Trade and Industrial Education, works with the teachers of Vocational Trade Education in the high schools.

James T. Taylor, retired professor of psychology at North Carolina College, was appointed in 1963 by Governor Sanford to serve on the State Employment Security Commission. His function is to encourage young people to acquire the necessary educational experience and skills to fit them for self-supporting citizenship . . . to make contacts with employers and attempts to encourage them to employ Negroes in their establishments and to grade them on the basis of merit and qualifications rather than upon race or color.

Frank A. Toliver has been a supervisor of Secondary Education since 1958. He had been a successful high school principal at Ashe-

MRS. GEORGIA BARBEE
Health Educator

MRS. DORIS L. BROWN
Supervisor of School Libraries

MRS. LOIS BROWN
Area Supervisor, School Lunch
Program

W. T. JOHNSON, SR.
Western District Supervisor
Vocational Agriculture

ville and is well trained for his position. Dr. Toliver's chief function is working with high school principals, aiding them in achieving accreditation and in maintaining standardization.

Mrs. Edna Trotter is one of the consultants with the State School lunch program.

J. W. Warren is the Eastern District Supervisor of Vocational Agriculture, working with teachers of Vocational Agriculture in the high schools of the eastern sections of the State.

Frank B. Weaver is one of the consultants in the field of Elementary Education. Says Dr. Weaver:

> As State Supervisor of Elementary Education, my greatest interest is to assist local school personnel in their efforts to insure a greater quantity and quality in the education of all North Carolina boys and girls. This necessitates constant vigilance to insure that teachers continually excite the minds and arouse the powers of their pupils.

Harold H. Webb is a consultant in Science Education. On the impact of science upon Quality Education, he writes:

> If to-day's children are to live in the twenty-first Century, they must have an understanding of the nature of science and its implication in the development of technology. Our public schools attempt to raise the level of scientific literacy among the population and give concern in stimulating the interest of pupils who may follow some aspect of science in choosing a career.

Miss Augusta W. White is an assistant supervisor of Home Economics Education, working with teachers of the subject in the high schools.

Mrs. Ruth L. Woodson has been with the State Department for many years, having succeeded Marie McIver who died in 1948. Mrs. Woodson came to the Department well recommended, as she had had superior training and a rich teaching experience.[12]

With such talent existing in this type of educational leadership at the State level, Negro children in the public schools can reasonably be expected to improve their performance and thus fulfill their responsibility in the requirements of Quality Education.

Closely allied to the professional leadership under the State Department and that of appointment by the Governor is the organized professional leadership of teachers which is definitely motivating Quality Education at high level function. The North Carolina Teachers Association is a cogent force in bolstering State and Local effort to achieve a high standard of performance among both pupils and teachers. Under the magnetic leadership of the late W. L. Greene, as Executive Secretary and Mrs. Hilda H. Fountain, as Chairman of the

---

[12] Interviews, N. C. State Department Officials

JOHN R. LARKIN
*Consultant for Negro
Welfare*

JAMES R. TAYLOR
*Assistant Supervisor and Teacher
Trainer of Vocational Trade and
Industrial Education*

JAMES T. TAYLOR
*Consultant, N. C. Employment
Security Commission*

FRANK A. TOLIVER
*State Supervisor, Secondary
Education*

169

Classroom Teachers Division, this group became the first Negro classroom Teachers association to become allied with the National Education Association.[13] In 1963, Mrs. Elizabeth D. Koontz, a classroom teacher at Price High School in Salisbury, was elected Vice President of the N.E.A. Department of Classroom Teachers, the first Negro teacher to be elected to so exalted a position.

In 1962, Dr. Charles A. Lyons, Jr., a former dean at Elizabeth City State College, was elected Executive Secretary of the N. C. Teachers Association, succeeding W. L. Greene who had served from 1943 to the time of his death in 1961.

Mrs. Edna C. Richards has been the Executive Secretary of the Department of Classroom Teachers of the N. C. Teachers Association since it was organized. Two new workers were appointed to the Headquarters staff in 1963: Miss Barbara Hankins and Fred D. McNeill, Jr.

Mr. McNeill succeeds W. I. Morris as Field Representative. His chief function is to work with state and local leaders in coordinating professional activities of the membership in the N. C. Teachers Association.

Miss Hankins' position is an added one — Coordinator of Publications, Public Relations, and Research. From the Editor of the N. C. Teachers Record are these words relative to Miss Hankins:

> At ease in the field of creative and journalistic writing, and a co-contributor of a forth-coming publication of critical essays, Miss Hankins comes to the N. C. Teachers Association qualified and anxious to do the work before her.[14]

The N. C. Teachers Association gives liberal opportunities for leadership in the District program set up by H. V. Brown in 1936 and in the expanded program of the Daniels Plan set up by Dr. R. P. Daniel in 1949. Aside from the eight districts now in operation (1963) the functions of the N. C. Teacher Association cover every field of public education with programs aimed to achieve high quality performance in each. It reaches into the activities of the local units giving to every teacher identified with it ample opportunity of democratic expression and opportunity to select the officials of the State Association by voting in their individual units.

The N. C. Teachers Association has always endeavored to maintain a high standard of professional motivation and has been led by men and women thoroughly imbued with educational acumen. Since 1922, the year of the great bulge in membership, the following have

---

[13] Brown, *History of Education of Negroes*, p. 121.

[14] *N. C. Teachers Record*, October, 1963; p. 7.

J. W. WARREN
Eastern District Supervisor
Vocational Agriculture

FRANK B. WEAVER
State Supervisor, Elementary
Education

HAROLD H. WEBB
Consultant, Science Program

MRS. RUTH LAWRENCE WOODSON
State Supervisor, Elementary
Education

served as president: James E. Shepard of Durham, S. G. Atkins of Winston-Salem, W. S. Turner of Raleigh, G. E. Davis of Charlotte, O. R. Pope of Rocky Mount, J. H. Bias of Elizabeth City, Charlotte Hawkins-Brown of Sedalia, Rose Aggrey of Salisbury, J. W. Seabrook of Fayetteville, H. L. Trigg of Raleigh (at the time of his election), J. A. Tarpley of Greensboro, James T. Taylor of Durham, H. V. Brown of Goldsboro, A. H. Anderson of Winston-Salem, C. L. Blake of Charlotte, Ida H. Duncan of Salisbury, S. D. Williams of Elizabeth City, C. J. Barber of Garner, W. R. Collins of Smithfield, and Lafayette Parker of Winston-Salem (elected in 1962).[15]

The official organ of the Association, the *N. C. Teachers Record,* was first published in 1932 and is issued four times a year. It is a well edited and a valuable record of information. Copies of this publication are bound and filed in the office of the Executive Secretary. The Association also publishes a "News-Letter" containing detailed information of interest to all teachers of the State.

Leaving the professional emphasis upon Quality Education, let us consider the impact of some practical applications of the subject. In the previous chapter some mention was made of the relationship of Negro students with the industrial education program, (The I. E. C. — Industrial Education Centers). It was pointed out from surveys that Negroes are now afforded opportunity to pursue training in these centers. However, in comparison with the number of whites enrolled in the centers, the reports show the enrollment of Negroes tragically low. The causes of this disparity are a lack of interest in some instances and a lack of certain technical skills in others which preclude admission of Negroes in larger numbers.

It is in circumstances like these causes that Quality Education among Negroes meets its greatest test: viz., failure to create a vision of the inevitable and lack of fitting the student with adequate skills and a sufficient supply of useful knowledge. School administrators, supervisors, and teachers are growing increasingly aware of this charge and are resolved to meet it, but unless and until that awareness has become contagious among the pupils and they, too, resolve to meet it, there will be little improvement shown.

The above inference is not meant to imply that educational effort is designed for admission to the Industrial Education Centers only, but it does mean to assert that that apathy discovered toward interest in the industrial trend and the negative attitudes toward protracted study run parallel and are the very nemesis of Quality Education. No effort on the part of administrators and teachers can effect Quality Education until attitudes toward study become positive whether the choice is for industrial training or liberal arts college, or any other field of endeavor; the basic requirements are vision and preparation.

---

[15] Brown, *Op. Cit.,* p. 123; *N. C. Teachers Record,* October, 1963.

W. L. GREENE (Deceased)

Former Executive Secretary, N. C.
Teachers Association

CHARLES A. LYONS, JR.

Executive Secretary, N. C.
Teachers Association

MRS. EDNA C. RICHARDS
Executive Secretary N.C.T.A.
Classroom Teachers

MISS BARBARA J. HANKINS
Coordinator of Publications, Public
Relations, and Research, N.C.T.A.

MRS. ELIZABETH D. KOONTZ
Vice President, NEA Department
of Classroom Teachers

FRED D. MCNEILL, JR.
Field Representative, N. C.
Teachers Association

175

Some aspects of efforts on the part of administrators and teachers in two different institutions are illustrated as samples of what many other institutions are doing to awaken their students to potentialities which too often lie dormant.

The first is from Dudley High School in Greensboro, J. A. Tarpley, Principal. Says Dr. Tarpley:

> Dudley High does not look with favor upon granting diplomas to any person the quality of whose performance has been on a barely passing standard in all of the subjects studied. A graduate should reflect a reasonable degree of quality in academic achievement in at least one (or more) of the subjects pursued in high school.

Final grades are evaluated in terms of quality of the work which a student does in earning his mark. Following is a schedule of quality points which should encourage profound study among the students:

```
A  equals  4  quality  points
B    ”     3     ”        ”
C    ”     2     ”        ”
D    ”     1     ”        ”
```

No pupil, whose over-all average in quality points falls below 2.5 will be graduated. This means that a pupil who makes a "D" in one subject must make at least a "B" in another to off-set the "D."[16]

In a different type of approach is an objective program conducted at Dillard High School in Goldsboro: The Live Project. One of the first of the Negro schools to adopt the Trade and Industrial program was the high school of which the author was then principal, Dillard High School. Vocational training is not offered in lieu of academic work, but grows out of it. Under the instruction of H. B. Lucas in brick masonry and T. L. Parks in carpentry, both products of the Hampton philosophy of industrial education, the trade classes of Dillard High have constructed dwelling houses which, when completed, are sold at auction. These structures were erected under codes approved by local statutes just as if constructed by private contractors and have been adjudged by competent authority as excellent jobs.

Thus, through this type of objective training, the students of the Vocational Department are given every opportunity to combine comprehensive knowledge of certain areas and specific job skills based upon sound values of general education. These students spend three periods a day at trade education and the rest of the day at subjects which not only aid them in their trade work, but enable them to meet the requirements of high school graduation.

During the "G.I." program, following World War II, veterans

---

[16] Correspondence, J. A. Tarpley.

J. A. TARPLEY

*Principal, Dudley High School,
Greensboro*

were trained in brick masonry, carpentry, and in auto-mechanics and to-day are earning a livelihood from this objective program.[17]

These two aspects of Quality Education, though widely different examples, are types of effort which can be found among many of our schools which are endeavoring to awaken Negro students to a sense of need, preparation, and performance. Such awareness and dedication on the part of both teacher and pupil are the very essence of Quality Education.

No one in the State has been more keenly aware of the need for Quality Education as well as the need for a healthy economy for all people than the Governor of the State, Terry Sanford. Aside from having inspired educators to adopt the slogan, "Quality Education," Governor Sanford has injected other objective programs which make his actions prove his words. Consider: (1) his School for Gifted Children; (2) his Assault on Poverty; and (3) his efforts to eradicate the drop-out problem.

The idea of creating a special summer school program for gifted and talented children originated with the staff of Governor Sanford. The Governor submitted his proposal to the Carnegie Corporation of New York which in January 1963 awarded a matching grant of $225,000.00. Another $225,000.00 was donated by eleven foundations and industries in Winston-Salem. A total of $450,000.00 was assigned to finance the operation of an 8-weeks residential summer school program for 1963, 1964, and 1965 on the campus of Salem College in Winston-Salem.

The school opened with 400 children June 10, 1963. It is to the credit of a liberal-minded Governor and to the promoters of the project that it was opened and operated on a non-racial basis. Twenty-eight Negro children were included in the enrollment and the report from the Director states that they performed from "average to exceptional."

The primary objective is to provide a differential education for students with academic giftedness, artistic talent, or both. Three areas of learning were included, as follows:

The first is intended to give the students broad, advanced foundational knowledge in his area of greatest aptitude and interest.

The second is aimed at general intelligence development of the creative mind by probing into some of man's essential ideas and learning the nature of critical thought.

The third is designed to provide for self-expression in public performances which are artistic or intellectual in nature, and for cultural broadening by attending lectures, seminars, and artistic performances.

A fourth experience is offered by a recreational pro-

---

[17] Interview, H. B. Lucas, Instructor Building Trades, Dillard High School.

gram — both organized and impromptu — which provides students with relaxation, physical exercises, and a further opportunity to get to know one another in an informal atmosphere.

No grades nor credits are given, few assigned home lessons, but students are expected to work independently during free time. The primary aim is to provide gifted children with a foundation of knowledge and critical inquiry on which they can later build and develop into tomorrow's leaders.[18]

Assault on Poverty. The Governor has been equally concerned with the status of employment among Negroes. He has consistently urged that citizens end unfair discrimination in employment and give the Negro full chance to earn a decent living for himself and his family. Said Governor Sanford:

> The time has come for American citizens to abandon their reluctance to accept the Negro in employment.

He called upon State officials to formulate policies that will not exclude Negroes from state employment, thus opening new opportunities for Negro citizens which will add new economic growth for everybody. Continuing, he said:

> We can do this, we will do this — we will do it because our economy cannot afford to have so many people fully or partially unproductive. We will do it because it is honest and fair for us to give all men and women their best chance in life.[19]*

The Governor's "Assault on Poverty" described by Editor Kendall in his "Tar Heel Talk" is aimed at lifting North Carolina and assuring a richer, fuller life for oncoming generations. The first emphasis of this program was on the public school system as the State's Educational Foundation. The major attention shifted to more strongly buttressed and adequate higher education as furthered by the reorganization measure enacted by the 1963 General Assembly. The next logical step was concern for seeing that these educational opportunities are made available or taken to the people who need them — both to the gifted as well as to the disadvantaged child. Said Governor Sanford:

> We have areas in our country in every state, in every city where families have been either cut off from or overwhelmed by the forward rush of our Society, and their children are handicapped.

These are children of poverty, the children of remote and

---

[18] Brochure, *The Governor's School for Gifted and Talented Children.*

*Mention has already been made of the appointment of Mrs. Herbin to consult with Governor Sanford with regard to the employment of Negroes.

[19] *N. C. Teachers Record,* January, 1963; p. 5.

undeveloped mountains, cove, children of the tenant land and worst of all, the children of the city slums — the benighted, deprived, the blighted children.

The schools in which such children find themselves must be adapted to the children's needs. It does no credit to a school today to say that it has learning available and it is the child's fault if he does not learn.

The Ford Foundation made a multi-million dollar grant for the Governor's program, "Assault on Poverty."[20] Let it be hoped that the "powers-that-be" will support the Governor in taking advantage of this most salutary philanthropy.

A third great concern of the Governor has been the vexing problem of keeping children in school until they graduate. One of the greatest obstacles to Quality Education, with which the State must contend is the "drop-out" problem. The inception of this problem is in a early negative attitude toward attendance, the responsibility for which must be charged to the home.

The 1963 General Assembly provided attendance regulations by appropriating funds for 150 counselors to combat poor attendance. This was the first time in fifty years that any machinery for the enforcement of attendance laws appeared on the statute books. However, only 68 of the 150 for which the funds were provided had been appointed for the 1963-64 school term. Sixteen of the twenty-seven districts in eastern counties, where the drop-out problem is most serious were without officials charged with enforcement.

There exists in these districts a continuation of the callousness, irresponsibility and inherent opposition to compulsory attendance which have been responsible for the State's illiteracy and ignorance. If only a half-way job is done in accepting the State's provision for attendance counselors, it should be done in those districts where it is needed most.[21]

A pilot program on ways and means to keep youth in school until graduation is being explored by the Guilford County Committee on Improved Attendance. A committee of 40 members, representing a cross section of business, industry, and labor, educators and legal activities has been formed to promote the program in Greensboro, High Point, and in rural Guilford Communities.[21] Prospects of its success will be sought in the immediate years ahead. Other communities might profit by this effort.

Conclusion

The story in this chapter has had its inference almost wholly upon public school emphasis toward Quality Education, but it would be far from fair to omit the fact that throughout our State's educa-

---

[20] Editorial, *Greensboro Daily News*, October 13, 1963.

[21] *Ibid.*, October 26, 1962; p. B-1.

tional endeavors are other valuable and important influences equally interested and actually engaged in the promotion of Quality Education and are playing significant roles in elevating the standard of citizenship.

There are the colleges, both private and State controlled, taxed to their capacities in enrollment and often inhibited by lack of funds, yet are yearly sending out well trained citizens to bolster the State's supply of teachers as well as professional people to improve the cultural life of the State. There are the Nurse Training institutions which are giving the State its fine ambassadors of mercy in their administrations to the ill. Finally, there is that great objective program of education among both adults and youth, the Farm and Home Extension service so important in elevating the standard of life on the farm and in the home.

All of these influences, from our beneficent Governor who guides the "Ship of State" to the humblest pupil who "burgeons" out the best there is in him — all working with dedication can make Quality Education a reality and thus prove North Carolina, the Grandest State in the Union.

R. E. JONES
State Agent, Extension Service
State Agriculture Agent, Extension Service

MRS. MINNIE MILLER BROWN
State Home Economics Agent, Extension Service

MRS. ELIZABETH BRIGHT BROWN

Wayne County Home Economics Agent — Extension Service
Wife of the author

Adams Elementary School — Wilson, North Carolina

North Everette School — Martin County

W. A. Robinson School — Pitt County

Addenda

To those who might wonder what influence the N. C. Teachers Association has had upon the emphasis of Quality Education, a facsimile of the program of the Thirty-First Annual Session of the N. C. Teachers Association held at A&M College (now A&T College) on June 13-17, 1911 is submitted below.

The list of names included on this program should strike a note of nostalgia in the minds of many veteran and retired teachers who read this program.

TUESDAY, JUNE 13, 1911 — 8:00 A.M.

Welcome, Behalf of College A&M .... Dr. J. D. Chavis

Welcome, Behalf of Public Schools .... Miss Edna E. Mitchell

Response

Remarks

WEDNESDAY, JUNE 14 — 9:00-12:00

Primary Work .... Supervisor, Miss Julia Amee, *Principal*
Garfield Graded School, Raleigh

How to Teach Reading .... Miss Lucille McLendon
Brick School, Enfield

Language .... Miss Mattie M. Brown
Peabody Academy, Troy

Geography .... Miss Effie Reed
Asheboro

Writing .... Miss L. M. Jordan
Raleigh

Supervision of Negro Schools .... Professor C. L. Coon
Superintendent, Wilson

General Discussion

2:00-4:00 P.M.

Grammar School Work .... Professor C. A. Johnson
Oxford

Arithmetic .... Prof. T. J. Johnson, *Principal*
Graded School, Mt. Airy

History .... Professor R. W. Brown
Graded School, Winston-Salem

Reading and Spelling .... Mrs. L. M. Hunter
Raleigh

Address .... Professor J. A. Bivins
State Supervisor, Teacher Training

8:00 P.M.

President's Address .... Reverend G. C. Shaw
Principal, Mary Potter Seminary, Oxford

THURSDAY, JUNE 15 — 9:00-12:00

What are the Graded Schools doing to Educate
Our People? .... Professor J. A. McRae
Principal, Graded School, Asheboro

What Are the Women's Clubs Doing to Educate
Our People? .... Miss A. F. Ruffin
State Normal, Winston-Salem

What is the Educational Outlook of the
Counties? .... Miss Charlotte Hawkins
Principal, Sedalia High School

What is the Relation of Newspapers to Our
Educational Life? .... R. H. Adams
Henderson

Address .... Dr. James Hardy Dillard
Agent, Slater and Jeanes Funds

General Discussion

2:00-4:00 P.M.

What is the State Doing Through its Normals? —
Principal P. W. Moore, *Elizabeth City*
Principal E. E. Smith, *Fayetteville*
Principal F. M. Kennedy, *Winston-Salem*

What is the State Doing for Our Deaf and Dumb? ... Dr. A. W. Pegues
Principal D. D. & B. Institute, Raleigh

The Value of Education in Civic Life .... Dr. O. Faduma
Principal, Peabody Academy, Troy

THURSDAY — 8:30 P.M.

Address — Some Phases of Education .... Honorable J. Y. Joyner
State Superintendent, Public Instruction, Raleigh

FRIDAY, JUNE 16 — 9:00-12:00

Sanitation .... Dr. J. E. Dellinger
Greensboro

186

Address — The Place and Value of a Sincere Study of
Literature in Course of Study .... Dr. G. E. Davis
Biddle University, Charlotte

Address .... Professor W. T. B. Williams
Agent, Slater Fund

What is the Negro Doing to Help Educate Himself?

(a) Parochial Schools .... Dr. C. S. Brown
Principal, Waters Normal Institute, Winton
J. A. Fennell, *Principal*
Burgaw High School, Burgaw

(b) College .... Dr. C. F. Meserve, *President*
Shaw University, Raleigh

Echoes from the Field

2:00-4:00

Reports of Committees

Election

EVENING SESSION

Grand Concert and Reception

Adjournment

OFFICERS

President .... G. C. Shaw, *Principal, Mary Potter, Oxford*

Vice President .... J. A. Cotton, *Principal, Henderson Institute*

Secretary .... J. W. Paisley, *Slater State Normal*

EXECUTIVE COMMITTEE

T. S. Inborden, *Bricks*

J. B. Dudley, *Principal, A&M College, Greensboro*

P. W. Moore, *Principal, State Normal, Elizabeth City*

C. H. Boyer, *Saint Augustine's College*

J. H. Branch, *Principal, Washington Graded School, Raleigh*

C. G. O'Kelley, *Vice President, National Training School, Durham*

J. A. Cotton, *Principal, Henderson Institute*

Index

Brinkley, Clotee 91
Brinn, A. L. 77
Broadhurst, Edgar D. 88
Brochies, Anna (Miss) 77
Brochett, John 91
Brochett, M. E. (Miss) 77
Brooks, E. C. 13, 95, 99, 100, 103, 104, 106, 107, 108, 109, 110, 111, 112, 114, 123, 127, 137
Broughton, Melville (Governor) 126
Brown, Anna 44
Brown, C. S. 52, 75, 187
Brown, Charlotte Hawkins (Dr.) 172, 186
Brown, Doris L. (Mrs.) 136, 166
Brown, Hiram 53
Brown, H. V. 170, 172
Brown, J. W. 68
Brown, James L. 89
Brown, Louise 91
Brown, Louise M. (Miss) 77
Brown, Lois (Mrs.) 136, 166
Brown, L. V. 92
Brown, Elizabeth B. (Mrs.) 183
Brown, Mattie M. (Miss) 185
Brown, Minnie Miller (Mrs.) 182
Brown, R. W. 185
Brunswick, County of 29, 52
Bryan, Walter C. 92
Bryant, D. W. 44
Bryant, James 44
Buchram School 53
Buncombe, County of 52
Burford, S. E. 129
Burgaw, City of 187
Burgaw High School 187
Burgaw Normal 53
Butler, J. H. 58
Butler, John H. M. 60
Bynum, James H. 87
Byrd, John W. 54
Byrd, W. A. 77
Byuarm, Samuel W. 158

Cabarrus, County of 26, 52
Cain, (Biblical Character) 11
Cain, Susan 44
Caldwell, Governor 31
Campaign for Education 82, 83, 84, 107
Congress of Colored Parents and Teachers 122
Cannady, Robert 54
Carnegie Corporation 178
Carney, Mable (Miss) 121
Carroll, Charles F. 13, 14, 131, 133, 141, 145, 154, 161
Carson, A. A. 57
Carter, J. A. 130
Carteret, County of 24, 53
Carthage, City of 35, 45

Cartwright, C. M. 53
Cartwright, R. R. 68, 76
Cary, City of 86
Chalmers, Thomas 44
Chambers, Junius L. 144
Chance, Julius C. 89
Chapel Hill, City of 27, 143
Charlotte, City of 25, 26, 35, 51, 88, 129, 142, 187
Charlotte Democrat (Newspaper) 17
Charlotte-Mecklenberg School System 143
Chavis, J. D. 185
Cheatham, H. P. 55
Cheatham, L. S. (Mrs.) 55
Chestnut, A. J. (Jr.) 44
Chestnut, Charles W. 45
Christmas, L. T. 53, 56
Civil Rights 12, 34, 138, 139
Civil War 11, 17, 30
Classroom Teachers Asso. 170
Claxton, P. P. 109
Clay, County of 28
Clayton, City of 54
Clayton Preparatory 54
Clements, Fannie (Miss) 57
Clement, George C. (Bishop) 107
Clemons, J. J. 52, 53
Cleveland, Grover (President) 62
Clinton, City of 143
Clinton Normal 52
Clumsford, (Township) 24
Coakley, Rosetta E. (Miss) 56
Coerr, Charles T. 53
Cofield, H. F. (Mrs.) 181
Cohoon, F. F. 65
College Street School (Asheville) 52
Collins, Jennie 44
Collins, Rufus 44
Collins, W. R. 172
Colored Normal (See Fayetteville State Normal; State Teachers College)
Coltrane, W. H. 87
Columbia University 121
Columbus, County of 91
Compulsory Education (See Attendance, Compulsory)
Conant, James B. 156, 157
Concord, City of 51
Connet, Alfred (Reverend) 53
Coon, C. L. 76, 185
Cooper, Aaron 55
Cooper, A. B. 52
Cooper, Thomas C. 77, 91
Cordon, J. E. (Reverend) 76
Cornell University 60
Corprew, E. H. 76
Correll, H. 56
Cotten, Charles 44
Cotten, W. J. 44
Cotton, J. A. 187

193

194

196